The Faraway Nearby

Rebecca Solnit

GRANTA

Copyright page tk

The Faraway Nearby

Also by Rebecca Solnit

Secret Exhibition: Six California Artists of the Cold War Era

Savage Dreams: A Journey into the Landscape Wars of the American West

A Book of Migrations: Some Passages in Ireland

Wanderlust: A History of Walking

Hollow City: The Siege of San Francisco and the Crisis of American Urbanism (with Susan Schwartzenberg)

As Eve Said to the Serpent: On Landscape, Gender, and Art

River of Shadows: Eadweard Muybridge and the Technological Wild West

Hope in the Dark: Untold Histories, Wild Possibilities

A Field Guide to Getting Lost

Yosemite in Time: Ice Ages, Tree Clocks, Ghost Rivers (with Mark Klett and Byron Wolfe)

Storming the Gates of Paradise: Landscapes for Politics

A Paradise Built in Hell: The Extraordinary Communities That Arise in Disaster

Infinite City: A San Francisco Atlas

for the mothers

and the wolves

Contents

The Faraway Nearby

1 · Apricots

What's your story? It's all in the telling. Stories are compasses and architecture; we navigate by them, we build our sanctuaries and our prisons out of them, and to be without a story is to be lost in the vastness of a world that spreads in all directions like arctic tundra or sea ice. To love someone is to put yourself in their place, we say, which is to put yourself in their story, or figure out how to tell yourself their story.

Which means that a place is a story, and stories are geography, and empathy is first of all an act of imagination, a storyteller's art, and then a way of traveling from here to there. What is it like to be the old man silenced by a stroke, the young man facing the executioner, the woman walking across the border, the child on the roller coaster, the person you've only read about, or the one next to you in bed?

We tell ourselves stories in order to live, or to justify taking lives, even our own, by violence or by numbness and the failure to live; tell ourselves stories that save us and stories that are the quicksand in which we thrash and the well in which we drown, stories of justification, of accursedness, of luck and star-crossed love, or versions clad in the cynicism that is at times a very elegant garment. Sometimes the story collapses, and it demands that we recognize we've been lost, or terrible, or ridiculous, or just stuck; sometimes change arrives like an ambulance or a supply drop. Not

Moths drink the tears of sleeping birds. This is the title of a short scientific report

a few stories are sinking ships, and many of us go down with these ships even when the lifeboats are bobbing all around us.

In *The Thousand and One Nights,* known in English as *The Arabian Nights,* Scheherazade tells stories in order to keep the sultan in suspense from night to night so he will not kill her. The backstory is that the sultan caught his queen in the embrace of a slave and decided to sleep with a virgin every night and slay her every morning so that he could not be cuckolded again. Scheherazade volunteered to try to end the massacre and did so by telling him stories that carried over from one night to the next for nights that stretched into years.

She spun stories around him that kept him in a cocoon of anticipation from which he eventually emerged a less murderous man. In the course of all this telling she bore three sons and delivered a labyrinth of stories within stories, stories of desire and deception and magic, of transformation and testing, stories in which the action in one freezes as another storyteller opens his mouth, pregnant stories, stories to stop death.

We think we tell stories, but stories often tell us, tell us to love or to hate, to see or to be blind. Often, too often, stories saddle us, ride us, whip us onward, tell us what to do, and we do it without questioning. The task of learning to be free requires learning to hear them, to question them, to pause and hear silence, to name them, and then to become the storyteller. Those ex-virgins who died were inside the sultan's story; Scheherazade, like a working-class hero, seized control of the means of production, and talked her way out.

Sometimes the key arrives long before the lock. Sometimes a story falls in your lap. Once about a hundred pounds of apricots fell into

from 2006, and the moths are a species on the island of Madagascar named

mine. They came in three big boxes, and to keep them from crushing each other under their weight or from rotting in close quarters, I spread them out on a sheet on the plank floor of my bedroom. There they presided for some days, a story waiting to be told, a riddle to be solved, and a harvest to be processed. They were an impressive sight, a mountain of apricots in every stage from hard and green to soft and browning, though most of them were that range of shades we call apricot: pale orange with blushes of rose and yellow-gold zones, upholstered in a fine velvet, not as fuzzy as peaches, not as smooth as plums. The ripe ones had the faint sweet perfume particular to that fruit.

I had expected them to look like abundance itself and they looked instead like anxiety, because every time I came back there was another rotten one or two or three or dozen to cull, and so I fell to inspecting the pile every time I passed by instead of admiring it. The reasons why I came to have a horde of apricots on my bedroom floor are complicated. They came from my mother's tree, from the home she no longer lived in, in the summer when a new round of trouble began.

Two summers before the apricots, my mother had begun to get confused, to get lost, to lock herself out of her own house, to have serial emergencies that often prompted her to call me for a rescue or a solution. She had memorized my phone number decades before; my three brothers lived no further away, but they had other area codes and newer numbers, and she had always hidden her troubles from them. They were the audience for her best self, for who she wished to be seen as, and I was stationed backstage, where things were messier.

I told my middle and younger brothers that we needed to make

Hemiceratoides hieroglyphica, *but the title is a sentence, and the sentence reads*

it a group effort, because if this chaos remained my mother's and my secret, as most of her illnesses and complaints had been before, it could consume me. These brothers did a lot for her in other ways; they stepped up, and the burden was shared, but all her emergency calls still came to me. One day I asked her why she always called me and not them. "Well, you're the girl," she said, then added, "and you're just sitting around the house all day doing nothing anyway." That was one way to describe the life of a writer.

She lost her car, and I went over and drove her around until we found it; we crossed our fingers until she lost her driver's license for good; she lost her purse and I turned her house upside down until it showed up on the seat of a chair pushed into a desk days after we'd given up; she lost her keys or her wallet, and we came over and unlocked the door with our keys and made more keys and left one with her nearby friend, and hid one on the premises, and then a replacement, and then one after that. I never knew when the phone would ring with an emergency and when the phone didn't ring, I worried about whether she was in such dire straits that she didn't even have access to a phone or the capacity to use it. I was constantly on edge, waiting for the next crisis.

We kept trying to prop her up at home. I put a hook behind the front door to hang her purse on so she'd know where it was, but she wouldn't use it, and she took my proposal to reduce her nine or so purses to one badly; she liked the big red luggage tag I put on the key to the front door until she lost it, and then a series of highly visible successors, and appreciated the list of essential phone numbers I pinned to the wall, but she called up and cursed me the day I borrowed her address book so I could make a large

like a ballad of one line or a history compressed down to its barest essentials.

copy bound in red with a ribbon on it to tether to furniture or dangle out of piles.

The copy got lost too, but not as often, and I had another photocopy to back up the backup, in the day when she still read and used phones and kept up with friends. I bought a corded telephone that wouldn't get lost or drained of power the way the cordless ones did, but couldn't ensure it would be hung up in between calls, and, because she couldn't learn how to punch in the time on modern microwave keypads, I found an old dial-operated microwave, like the one she'd burned out by setting it to heat something for hours instead of minutes. I found a pretty chain for her eyeglasses and then another one and helped her get more pairs of glasses.

Like many elderly people, she was convinced that, rather than her losing things, others were stealing them—irons, purses, keys, laundry, money—and she lost more things by hiding them from these fictitious characters who helped conceal her real problems. The world of her imagination filled up with thieves and prowlers, though she'd never actually been the victim of a crime in that nice neighborhood twenty miles north of the city. She was afraid of people peering in the window and had most of them entirely covered, so that she would live by lamplight on a blazing blue and gold July day.

She tried to take the bus to see a friend who was having a birthday and got off at the wrong stop and took, so far as I could tell, a long hike across the shoulder of the small mountain between two towns and then got rides from passersby, none of whom bothered to take her all the way, and ended up home. She reported on it blithely, as an adventure, but a few years before, two elderly

There are two protagonists in it, a sleeper and a drinker, a giver and a taker, and

sisters she knew had gotten lost on a hike in her county. I can't remember if one or both died of exposure before they were located. My middle brother ordered a medical alert bracelet with contact information on it and put it on her like a dog tag in those days when we were propping her up with devices and systems that would mostly fail anyway.

I composed an essay in my head somewhere in the midst of all these crises called "Shipwrecked on the Dark Continent" but never found time to write it. Taking care of the elderly comes without the vast literature of advice and encouragement that accompanies other kinds of relationships, notably romantic love and childbearing. It sneaks up on you as something that is not supposed to happen, or rather you crash into this condition that you have not been warned about, a rocky coast not on the map. In the preferred stories the last years of life are golden and the old all ripen into wisdom, not decay into diseases that mimic mental illness and roll backward into chaotic childhood and beyond. My mother had always wanted me to take care of her, but she pictured this as a manifestation of her ascendancy, not her decline.

We took her to doctors who treated us like delinquent parents for letting her live alone, though it wasn't up to us and we were trying to change the situation. They offered prescriptions but no advice on how to get her to take a pill twice a day when she didn't know what day it was and what she'd done ten minutes ago. I tried a wall calendar with crack baggies containing the day's prescriptions stapled to each day, but she never looked at the calendar. That was the era of patching and bailing the sinking boat.

We floundered through a few grueling years of these crises while I mounted a low-key campaign to convince her that leaving

---

what are tears to the former is food to the latter. The story tells us everything we

her suburban home of thirty years would be a boon. I'd point out that if she lived in a building with a manager, she would never have to wait for someone to drive out from another county to unlock her door, and that it would be more sociable. She was lonely too, with her driver's license taken away, her old friends dying or distancing themselves or at the other end of a lost or dead telephone, with the necessary phone numbers in the missing phone book.

Finally, at the beginning of the apricot summer, we moved her to a charming independent-living senior apartment complex near my two relevant brothers and still a bridge away from me, and things began falling apart in earnest. When we'd moved her from her dark, disheveled home we'd pried her loose from a map of familiar routines and layouts, within which she had been able to cope by habit. Or perhaps we hadn't realized the extent to which she had not been coping.

When we packed her home up, I found fruit decomposing in dark cupboards, a trivet for hot dishes in her sock drawer, family photographs and her wedding pictures in the other clothing drawers, and wads of bills cached in all kinds of hiding places and fallen behind bureaus, and chaotic piles and tangles everywhere. The new place was just a studio apartment, and it justified simplifying her possessions down to essentials. She saw this as taking her things away, when she wasn't regarding the new place as a temporary lodging, a hotel, from which she'd return to her old territory.

She never got a new map into her head, never learned the way to the grocery store half a block away on the other side of the street or the layout of the building or even her own apartment. She couldn't. Even crossing the street was dangerous, both because she

ever wanted a story to tell. There is difference. There is contact. You can feed on

wasn't looking for cars and because once she got to the other side she'd have no idea how she got there or where she was. My younger brother believed ardently in protecting her dignity and autonomy, but being hit by a car is undignified. We arrived at a new level of crisis that required one of us to be with her during all waking hours. Then we hired aides to supplement us until we moved her to the residential care facility with the bucolic name where she was supposed to be fully cared for and safe.

They misled us about their capacity to cope and took a lot of money they weren't going to return, and whenever things didn't go smoothly they passed the burden to us. We went back to spending long chunks of time with her and hiring one-on-one caregivers. She became a geriatric delinquent, prone to lashing out and running away. We tried to forestall her solo expeditions by taking her on a long walk every morning through the pleasant residential streets with their burgeoning flower gardens. Since the rest of my conversations with her were chaotic or perilous, I talked to her mostly about the colors of the houses and about irises, honeysuckle, nasturtiums, passionflowers, sunflowers, morning glories, and the other plants we passed on those walks.

In Alzheimer's disease the hippocampus is among the areas affected first, that little coil in the central core of the brain that shares a Latin name with sea horses. Shaped like a sea horse, it forms memories. As the hippocampus erodes, the sufferer loses the ability to form new memories but hangs on to existing ones at first. Then the neocortex, that overmantle of the brain that hosts much of our intellectual functioning, begins to deteriorate. The neocortexes of many animals are comparatively smooth and

sorrow. Your tears are delicious. Moths drink the tears of sleeping birds. The

simple, but the human neocortex is intricately crenelated to create a huge amount of surface area within the confines of the skull.

Think of the brain as an intricate landscape of canyons, arroyos, inlets, bays, tunnels, and escarpments surrounding a buried sea horse, with the neurons that relay information scattered all through—scientists call this the "neuron forest." In the disease that was in my mother's brain, these nerve cells become tangles, as though the forest has been overtaken by the kind of vines you sometimes see creeping up a tree to strangle it. Other parts go blank; the trees die off, and the ventricles that run through the brain enlarge like streams becoming canals. The landscape in which character and capacity are grounded is metamorphosing profoundly, irrevocably. Eventually it erodes; the brain actually shrinks.

They say that Alzheimer's mimics childhood run in reverse, but children's voracious minds are seizing on the knowledge that's disintegrating at the other end of life, and the conditions are as dissimilar as gaining and losing. I thought of my mother as a book coming apart, pages drifting away, phrases blurring, letters falling off, the paper returning to pure white, a book disappearing from the back because the newest memories faded first, and nothing was being added. The words were beginning to vanish from her speech, leaving blank spots behind.

It was in the midst of that crisis that my younger brother, who was in charge of preparing her house for sale, decided that he needed to strip her apricot tree of all its fruit. It was a gesture of salvage, of anxiety, and of generosity. She had planted the tree decades earlier, and it had flourished. I don't recall ever eating an apricot from it before the great mound came to me, though there

sentence can run away with you until you have forgotten science and the lack

is a picture of me in my twenties, my feet planted on a couple of bare boughs, pruning shears in hand, looking at ease up there.

I wrote that and then went to pull the faded Polaroid out of a box and found that actually I was standing atop a tall ladder next to the tree with something unrecognizable in my hand. It was my younger brother in the companion snapshot who was standing in the apricot tree itself with the pruning shears. Memory, even in the rest of us, is a shifting, fading, partial thing, a net that doesn't catch all the fish by any means and sometimes catches butterflies that don't exist. After all, I had turned myself into my brother when I tried to remember the photographs. Twenty years later, he must have gone up a ladder himself to get all the fruit, every last one on the apricot tree. He gave some of the harvest to others, but the lion's share came to me.

Every time I looked at the mound of apricots there were a few more going bad that needed to be culled before the decay spread. The pile began to look like an organism, a human-size entity with a life of its own, the occupying army in my bedroom. Juices began to ooze out, as though I had a corpse decomposing on my floor, while the rest remained sweet, ripening in a rush as I waited for a window of time to do something with them.

The fruit on my floor made me start to read fairy tales again. They are full of overwhelming piles and heaps that need to be contended with, the roomful of straw the poor girl in "Rumpelstiltskin" needs to spin into gold overnight, the thousand pearls scattered in the forest moss the youngest son needs to gather in order to win the princess, the mountain of sand to be moved by teaspoon. The heaps are only a subset of the category of impossible

of sorrow in the tears of birds—in this case magpie robins and

tasks that include quests, such as gathering a feather from the tail of the firebird who lives at the end of the world, riddles, and facing overwhelming adversaries.

A cruel fairy named Magotine gives an accursed queen cobwebs to spin into thread, a mountain to climb with a millstone around her neck, a pitcher full of holes to fill with the water of discretion, tasks she must complete if the green serpent to whom she's married is to be turned back into a human being. Such tasks are always the obstacles to becoming, to being set free, or finding love. Carrying out the tasks undoes the curse. Enchantment in these stories is the state of being disguised, displaced in an animal's body or another's identity. Disenchantment is the blessing of becoming yourself.

This abundance of unstable apricots seemed to be not only a task set for me, but my birthright, my fairy-tale inheritance from my mother who had given me almost nothing since my childhood. It was a last harvest, a heap of fruit from a family tree, like the enigmatic gifts of fairy tales: a magic seed, a key to an unknown door, a summoning incantation. Bottling, canning, composting, freezing, eating, and distilling them was the least of the tasks they posed. The apricots were a riddle I had to decipher, a tale whose meaning I had to make over the course of the next twelve months as almost everything went wrong.

Fairy tales are about trouble, about getting into it and out of it, and trouble seems to be a necessary stage on the route of becoming. All the enchantments and glass mountains and pearls the size of houses and princesses beautiful as the day and talking birds and part-time serpents are distractions from the tough core of most of

Newtonia birds—and remembered your own tears and pictured an asymmetrical

the stories, the struggle to survive against adversaries, to find your place in your world, and to come into your own. Difficulty is always a school, though learning is optional.

Fairy tales are almost always the stories of the powerless, of youngest sons, abandoned children, orphans, of humans transformed into birds and beasts or otherwise enchanted away from their own selves and lives. Even princesses are chattel to be disowned or sold by fathers, punished by stepmothers, or claimed by princes, though they often assert themselves in between and are rarely as passive as the cartoon versions. Fairy tales are children's stories not in who they were made for but in their focus on the early stages of life, when others have power over you and you have power over no one.

In them, power is rarely the right tool for survival anyway. Rather the powerless thrive on alliances, often in the form of reciprocated acts of kindness—from beehives that were not raided, birds that were not killed but set free or fed, old women who were saluted with respect. Kindness sown among the meek is harvested in crisis, in fairy tales and sometimes in actuality. I know a man who lost a fortune suddenly and was penniless with a legal battle to fight and children to support. He found that he had another kind of wealth in the ties of affection and respect he had built up, wealth he would otherwise have never seen. Lawyers took on his case pro bono, the grocery store extended credit, the schools gave scholarships, and he got by on the wealth that was invisible before the money dried up.

In Hans Christian Andersen's retelling of the old Nordic tale that begins with a stepmother, "The Wild Swans," the banished sister can only disenchant her eleven exiled brothers—who are

relationship in which one sleeps and one is awake, one surrenders and one

swans all day but turn human at night—by gathering stinging nettles barehanded from churchyard graves, making them into flax, spinning them and knitting eleven long-sleeved shirts while remaining silent the whole time. If she speaks, they'll remain birds forever. In her silence she cannot protest the crimes she's accused of and is nearly burned as a witch.

Hauled off to the pyre as she knits the last of the shirts, she is rescued by the swans, who fly in at the last moment. As they swoop down, she throws the nettle shirts over them so that they turn into men again, all but the youngest brother whose shirt is missing a sleeve so that he's left with one arm and one wing, eternally a swan-man. Why shirts made of graveyard nettles by bleeding fingers and silence should disenchant men turned into birds by their stepmother is a question the story doesn't need to answer. It just needs to give us compelling images of exile, loneliness, affection, and metamorphosis—and of a heroine who nearly dies of being unable to tell her own story.

In those days my mother's condition felt like a fairy-tale curse that nothing could break, though it could be accommodated. The apricots, however, something could be done about. It wasn't that they were so hard to deal with as fruit, but that they seemed to invoke old legacies and tasks and to be an allegory, but for what?

acquires. One is being and the other doing. The moth is alert, at work, stealing

2 · Mirrors

That vast pile of apricots included underripe, ripening, and rotting fruit. The range of stories I can tell about my mother include some of each too. If I had written about her earlier, the story would have had the aura of the courtroom, for I had been raised on the logic of argument and fact and being right, rather than the leap beyond that might be love. I would have told it as a defendant, making my case against her to justify myself, who stood so long accused of so many sidelong things. Some of the urgency to be justified in my existence and to survive has fallen away, though the story remains, a hard pit after the emotion has gone.

There are other stories, not yet ripe, that I will see and tell in later years. Once the apricots arrived and I began thinking in fairy tales, I shocked myself by recalling the couplet from "Snow White," "Mirror, mirror, on the wall," because that conjunction of mothers and mirrors made me recognize how murderous my mother's fury was. She was devoured by envy for decades, an envy that was a story she told herself, a story of constant comparison.

She was a great believer in fairness. At her best she stood up for the rights of the oppressed and at the worst begrudged me anything I had that she thought she hadn't had. Envy was an emotion, and she turned her emotions into reasons and reasons into facts and believed facts were obdurate, unchangeable things, even as her emotions changed again and again. Those emotions metamorphosed

tears and flying through the night, because there is also night in this sentence, and

into stories and the stories she told herself summoned emotions apart from and long after the events.

Stories rode her, she was driven by stories—that beauty was the key to some happiness that had eluded her, that she had been done out of something that was rightfully hers, whether it was her mother's favor or her daughter's golden hair. Stories were a storm that blew her this way and that, but she believed in their truth and permanence—she had always been miserable, always happy, her life had been good, had been terrible, she had never said such a thing, felt such a thing, and though she brooded on slights for decades, she could never remember her own rage the day before.

My story is a variation on one I've heard from many women over the years, of the mother who gave herself away to everyone or someone and tried to get herself back from a daughter. Early on she assured me that she had measured me as a toddler, doubled my height, and deduced that I would be five foot two, seven inches shorter than her, when I grew up and that my hair—white blonde in my first years, lemon and then honey and then dirty blonde streaked by the sun with gold as I grew older—was going to turn brown at any moment.

This short, brown-haired daughter she decided upon was not terrifying, and she envisioned a modest future for me and occasionally tried to keep me to it. I remained a couple of inches shorter than her until her posture sagged, but she remained preoccupied with our relative heights. Once when I came over for a family dinner she seized me at the door and dragged me in front of a mirror to make sure she was still taller, and she called me "Shortie" well into the era of her Alzheimer's disease. It was my hair, however, that was her great grief.

wings of two kinds. As though the two characters were day and night itself, or as

Her dark hair had lovely russet undertones when she was young and turned white early. She dyed it light brown for a couple of decades before I convinced her to let it be. The first time I saw it white, when she was about sixty, I was astonished at her beauty, like a marble statue with blazing blue eyes. Having paler hair than mine changed nothing. She imagined blondeness as an almost supernatural gift, one that I had no right to receive since she had not, and she brought up my hair in countless unhappy ways over the years.

My hair was dyed, was brown, was unfair, was wrong, though there were a few years when she was angry about my eyebrows instead, beginning with a moment when I'd taken her out to breakfast and out of the blue she snapped, "It's not fair you got those eyebrows." Giving her breakfast did nothing, since I would not, could not, give her or give up my arched eyebrows or convince her that her own straight eyebrows were fine.

For mothers, some mothers, my mother, daughters are division and sons are multiplication; the former reduce them, fracture them, take from them, the latter augment and enhance. My mother, who would light up at the thought that my brothers were handsome, rankled at the idea that I might be nice-looking. The queen's envy of Snow White is deadly. It's based on the desire to be the most beautiful of all, and it raises the question of whose admiration she needs and what she thinks Snow White is competing for, this child whose beauty is an affliction. At the back of this drama between women are men, the men for whom the queen wants to be beautiful, the men whose attention is the arbiter of worth and worthlessness. There was nothing I could do, because there was nothing I had done: it was not my actions that triggered

if the drinker fed on the dreamer the way the moon reflects the light of the unseen

her fury, but my very being, my gender, my appearance, and my nonbeing—my failure to be the miracle of her completion and to be instead her division.

"Resentment is a storytelling passion," says the philosopher Charles Griswold in his book *Forgiveness*. I know well how compelling those stories are, how they grant immortality to an old injury. The teller goes in circles like a camel harnessed to a rotary water pump, diligently extracting misery, reviving feeling with each retelling. Feelings are kept alive that would fade away without narrative, or are invented by narratives that may have little to do with what once transpired and even less to do with the present moment. I learned this skill from my mother, though some of her stories were about me, and of course my perennial classics were about her. My father was destructive in a more uncomplicated, obvious way, but he is another story. Or maybe he is the misery at the root of my mother's behavior, and he certainly made her suffer, but there were people and historical forces at the root of his, and that line of logic goes on forever.

It wasn't only envy. When I was thirteen, my mother told me that the doctors had detected a lump in her breast. I found out decades later she had first told my father whose lack of sympathy over this was part of what precipitated their separation and protracted divorce. I didn't have much sympathy either; it was not that I refused to give it, but that there was none in my equipment yet, perhaps because I had experienced so little of it.

When she didn't get what she wanted from me that day she told me her medical news, she flew into a blasting fury that I remember, perhaps incorrectly, as the first of the long sequence of furies at what I was not or what she was not getting. I can still

sun. That moths drink the tears of sleeping birds is a template for many things; it

picture myself in front of the terrible house painted with the tan paint that had never dried properly so that a host of small insects stuck to it over the years. Now I can feel for that distressed woman who had no one compassionate to turn to, but at the time I just felt scorched and wronged. As it turned out, the lump was benign; the relationship, however, was malignant from then on.

Thereafter, she often visited her fury at others or at life upon me. She took pleasure in not giving me things that she gave to others, often in front of me, in finding ways to push me out of the group. She thought she would get something through these acts, and maybe she got a momentary sense of victory and power, and those were rare possessions for her. She didn't seem to know she also lost something through this strategy. In the decades that followed, I nursed her through other illnesses and injuries she kept secret from her sons, and during the worst of them, not so many years before the Alzheimer's arrived in force, she berated me for not feeling enough for her while I was tending her.

Sometimes it's valuable to return to the circumstances of childhood with an adult's resources and insights, and that time around I realized that I could not feel at all. Not for her, or for myself, except a dim horror, as if from a long way away. I had returned to the state in which I had spent my childhood, frozen, in suspended animation, waiting to thaw out, to wake up, waiting to live. I thought of her unhappiness as a sledge to which I was tethered. I dragged it with me and studied it in the hope of freeing myself and maybe even her.

She thought of me as a mirror but she didn't like what she saw and blamed the mirror. When I was thirty, in one of the furious letters I sometimes composed and rarely sent, I wrote, "You want

is a container of the familiar made strange, of sorrow turned into sustenance, of

me to be some kind of a mirror that will reflect back the self-image you want to see—perfect mother, totally loved, always right—but I am not a mirror, and the shortcomings you see are not my fault. And I can never get along with you as long as you continue demanding that I perform miracles."

I had brought her a copy of my first book and she responded by berating me for not visiting, though I had dropped it off late at night and knew that I would have been unwelcome at that hour. Had I visited at an earlier hour she would have found fault with something I'd done when I was with her. And had I not given her a copy, another failure could be charted. There was no winning, just some decisions about how to lose and how not to play. I have seen people with charismatic or charming parents forever hovering in hope of validation and recognition, and I wasn't waiting for those. I just wanted the war to end.

Long afterward I got asked over and over the most common and annoying question about Alzheimer's, whether she still recognized me. Recognition can mean so many things, and in some sense she had never known who I was. Much later, when she couldn't come up with my name or explain our relationship, I didn't care, since being recognized hadn't exactly been a boon. In that era, I think my voice and other things registered as familiar and set her at ease, and perhaps she knew me more truly. And perhaps I her, as so much that was superfluous was pared away and the central fact of her humanity and her vulnerability was laid bare.

Who was I all those years before? I was not. Mirrors show everything but themselves, and to be a mirror is like being Echo in the myth of Echo and Narcissus: nothing of your own will be

the myriad stories the natural world provides that are as uncannily resonant as

heard. The fact usually proffered about Narcissus is that he was in love with his own image in the mountain pool, but the more important one is that in his absorption in his reflection he lost contact with others and starved to death.

Glace, the French word for ice, can also mean mirror. Ice, mirror, glass: the glass coffin in which Snow White lies dormant, poisoned, might as well be made of ice, as though she were frozen like those bodies in cryogenic storage, waiting to be thawed when their disease becomes curable, or those mountaineers frozen into the ice at altitude. You freeze up in childhood, you go numb, because you cannot change your circumstances and to recognize, name, and feel the emotions and their cruel causes would be unbearable, and so you wait.

Ice, glass, mirrors. I was frozen, or rather thawing. I was a mirror, but my mother didn't like what she saw in it. I think of human psyches as landscapes and to the question of whether she was happy or unhappy, I think that others encountered her in a flower-spangled meadow that was highly cultivated, if not artificial, and I charted the authentic swamp of her unhappiness far away in another part of the landscape she herself did not care to know.

If my mother had chosen a fairy tale about herself, it would have been "Cinderella," the story of an overlooked, undervalued girl, a delicate child made into a workhorse. My mother's older sister was a lively girl off on her own pursuits; her younger sister was, in her account, the cosseted baby who grew up to look like her twin but was thought of—at least by my mother—as the pretty one. It was mostly confidence that made the younger girl take up eyebrow pencils and pretty dresses, while her older sister hung back; they were nevertheless close and fond.

any myth. The ancient Greeks used the word psyche *for breath, for life, for the*

From the time I was a small child, my mother would absent-mindedly call me by her little sister's name, so that I was cloaked in a jealousy and attachment that had been born more than a quarter century before me. My mother in her own stories was the freckled, skinny one on whom her mother leaned, the mother who sometimes kept her home from school because she was sickly, or for company, or to take care of her little sister. When my mother was ten, her mother returned to work because her building inspector husband died in a construction site accident, another abandonment for both of them.

If she was Cinderella, she was forever stuck in childhood, waiting for help, for transformation, stuck in situations that had ended half a century earlier, a Cinderella for whom no prince came, except her sons, the princes she made. She was self-conscious about her size-eleven feet and her height, bemoaning and boasting about the latter in turn. She had a strikingly pretty face, but beauty is as much a way of carrying yourself as physical attributes. She was thin-skinned, prim, unsure of herself, finicky, squeamish, anxious, and fretful, even as a child, in the stories told me.

Some instinct that comes from being at home in the world was never hers, the protective instinct that attracts you to what encourages you. Instead she was buffeted between principles and fears. She took the ought-to-be for the actual and adhered to what she should like and how things should be. It was as though she traveled by a map of the wrong place, hitting walls, driving into ditches, missing her destination, but never stopping or throwing out the map. And she never stopped being Cinderella, and told her own story largely as a series of things that happened to her rather than things she did.

vital essence of life, for the soul, and sometimes for butterflies that were the

The artist Ana Teresa Fernandez recently cast a pair of high-heeled shoes in ice and stood in the gutter of an inner-city street at night until they melted and left her barefoot and free. It was a battle between the warmth of her body and the coldness of the shoes, between her own fierce will and the imprisonment of the Cinderella story. The shoes were astonishingly beautiful, strange, alarming. They were shoes that wanted to kill your feet, shoes too brittle to walk in, shoes of the kind called stiletto, as though you could stab someone with them. In the two-hour video she compressed down to forty minutes or so of ordeal, they slowly disintegrated, like a story falling apart, like a belief wearing out, like a fear melting away.

When your feet or hands go numb with cold, they don't feel at all after a while. It's when they warm again that the pain begins, just as a limb hurts not when the blood flow ceases and it goes to sleep but when it wakes up. Tall, athletic Ana told me that it was when her feet began to thaw that the agony arrived. She endured the pain for the sake of a symbolic conquest of a pernicious story and for the sake of making a work of art that expressed her fierce feminism and brilliant imagination. In "Cinderella," women deform themselves to try to fit into the shoe; Ana destroyed the shoes, making something beautiful out of the war between flesh and ice, between a fairy tale that didn't fit and her own intransigent warmth. Not everyone has the will or the warmth.

Where does a story begin? The fiction is that they do, and end, rather than that the stuff of a story is just a cup of water scooped from the sea and poured back into it, but if I had to begin the story of my parents anywhere, it would be with my grandmothers, who were both motherless. Some secret of nurture withered a

emblem of the soul, though I wonder if a moth could also be a soul and if the

generation or two before I arrived, if it had ever existed before among the poor, marginalized people on the edges of Europe from whom I descend. Both my parents grew up with a deep sense of poverty that was mostly emotional but that they imagined as material long after they clambered into the middle class, and so they were more like a pair of rivalrous older siblings than parents who see their children as extensions of themselves and their hopes. They were stuck in separateness.

I didn't realize anything was odd until I was already on my own and found out that not everyone's parents cut them off financially as soon as the law allowed. I tried to leave home unsuccessfully at fourteen and fifteen and sixteen and did so successfully at seventeen, heading off to another country, as far away as I could go, and once I got there I realized I was more on my own than I had anticipated: I was henceforth responsible for myself, and thus began a few years of fairly dire poverty. For that odyssey my mother would not let me take any of the decent suitcases in her attic but gave me a huge broken one in which my few clothes and books tumbled like dice in a cup. My father gave me a broken travel clock that he said was worth repairing and I kept for years before I found that it was not. These were the gifts they sent me into the world with, which might be why the apricots from my mother's tree registered so strongly.

Like lawyers, writers seek consistency; they make a case for their point of view; they do so by leaving out some evidence; but let me mention the hundreds of sandwiches my mother made during my elementary school years, the peanut butter sandwiches I ate alone on school benches in the open, throwing the crusts into the air where the seagulls would swoop to catch them before they

Greek word encompasses them too. In the tale known as "Cupid and Psyche,"

hit the ground. When my friends began to have babies and I came to comprehend the heroic labor it takes to keep one alive, the constant exhausting tending of a being who can do nothing and demands everything, I realized that my mother had done all these things for me before I remembered. I was fed; I was washed; I was clothed; I was taught to speak and given a thousand other things, over and over again, hourly, daily, for years. She gave me everything before she gave me nothing.

It was in honor of that unremembered past that I took care of her, that and principle and compassion and solidarity with my brothers. How could I not? If my mother had been my arctic expedition, I was going to finish the journey. But after the peanut butter sandwiches, before the brain disease, it was hard to respond to her occasional generosities when the other side of her might show up at any moment, so she complained I was distant.

I was distant. I studied her, I pondered her. My survival depended on mapping her landscape and finding my routes out of it. We are all the heroes of our own stories, and one of the arts of perspective is to see yourself small on the stage of another's story, to see the vast expanse of the world that is not about you, and to see your power, to make your life, to make others, or break them, to tell stories rather than be told by them.

Perhaps another kind of daughter would have fought her to a truce or been utterly destroyed, and yet another thick-skinned enough to laugh it off or hardly notice rather than be caught up in the currents of emotion, though I can't imagine anyone emerging from those circumstances with the wisdom to negotiate a real peace early on. I coped by retreating and maybe I did become a mirror, a polished surface that shows nothing of what lies beneath.

Psyche is a wanderer whose odyssey begins when she is brought to her own

We were in a looking-glass world where I knew more about her childhood than she did about mine. When I was an adult, we didn't talk about me. If I told her something went wrong in my life, she was likely to focus on my mistakes or get upset and demand I reassure her fears. For an extended phase when I talked about something eventful in my own life, she would change the subject in the very opening words of her reply. So we talked about her, mostly about fears and grievances. When I'm most aggrieved, I feel most like her, with her sense of having been shorted, of being the victim, and not being her was always my goal. In this sense I saw, late in the game, I too was seeking to annihilate.

The autumn after the apricots, when everything was at its worst, I was asked to talk to a roomful of undergraduates in a university in a beautiful coastal valley. I talked about places, about the ways that we often talk about love of place, by which we mean our love for places, but seldom of how the places love us back, of what they give us. They give us continuity, something to return to, and offer a familiarity that allows some portion of our own lives to remain connected and coherent. They give us an expansive scale in which our troubles are set into context, in which the largeness of the world is a balm to loss, trouble, and ugliness. And distant places give us refuge in territories where our own histories aren't so deeply entrenched and we can imagine other stories, other selves, or just drink up quiet and respite.

The bigness of the world is redemption. Despair compresses you into a small space, and a depression is literally a hollow in the ground. To dig deeper into the self, to go underground, is sometimes necessary, but so is the other route of getting out of yourself,

funeral pyre in the mountains and abandoned there. In this tale that has all the

into the larger world, into the openness in which you need not clutch your story and your troubles so tightly to your chest. Being able to travel both ways matters, and sometimes the way back into the heart of the question begins by going outward and beyond. This is the expansiveness that sometimes comes literally in a landscape or that tugs you out of yourself in a story.

I used to go to Ocean Beach, the long strip of sand facing the churning Pacific at the end of my own city, for reinforcement, and it always put things in perspective, a term that can be literal too. The city turned into sand and the sand into surf and the surf into ocean and just to know that the ocean went on for many thousands of miles was to know that there was an outer border to my own story, and even to human stories, and that something else picked up beyond. It was the familiar edge of the unknown, forever licking at the shore.

I told the students that they were at the age when they might begin to choose places that would sustain them the rest of their lives, that places were more reliable than human beings, and often much longer-lasting, and I asked them where they felt at home. They answered, each of them, down the rows, for an hour, the immigrants who had never stayed anywhere long or left a familiar world behind, the teenagers who'd left the home they'd spent their whole life in for the first time, the ones who loved or missed familiar landscapes and the ones who had not yet noticed them.

I found books and places before I found friends and mentors, and they gave me a lot, if not quite what a human being would. As a child, I spun outward in trouble, for in that inside-out world, everywhere but home was safe. Happily, the oaks were there, the hills, the creeks, the groves, the birds, the old dairy and

hallmarks of what would become the classic fairy tales of female seekers, she

horse ranches, the rock outcroppings, the open space inviting me to leap out of the personal into the embrace of the nonhuman world.

Once when I was in my late twenties, I drove to New Mexico with my friend Sophie, a fierce, talented, young black-haired green-eyed whirlwind who had not yet found her direction. We had no trouble convincing ourselves it was worthwhile to drive the two days each way to New Mexico because there was a darkroom there that she could use to print photographs for a project we had. In those days we were exploring who we wished to become, what the world might give us, and what we might give it, and so, though we did not know it, wandering was our real work anyway.

I had discovered the desert west a few years before with the force of one falling in love and had learned something of how to enter it and move through it. I threw myself into the vastness whenever I could, and I began to have another life among the people of the desert who befriended me, and the places, and the illimitable sky that seemed like an invitation to open up and grow larger.

In those days I was finding my voice and my vocation and they were flourishing, but I was not yet hectic or pressured, and I found countless excuses to wander in that empty quarter of the continent, camping, visiting, working with Native American activists, discovering a world that demanded new senses and delivered wild gifts. We must have taken the most scenic route, because Marble Canyon was not on any imaginable direct route. It's the first canyon below Glen Canyon Dam, at the head of the Grand Canyon. We had driven through the flatlands and mountains of the Mojave, through the highs and lows of the Arizona desert, then

awakes alone in a palace. There an unknown, unseen lover visits her only at

past mesas and escarpments of red sandstone and spread out a tarp and slept on sand near the murmuring river that night and ate breakfast in the morning at the shady diner of the lodge up the road on that north side of the river.

At the long table next to us was a big exuberant group of people in their prime, talking and eating piles of food. I realized at some point they were a river-rafting party, and I must have spoken more loudly than I'd intended when I said that I'd give my eyeteeth to go down the Grand Canyon. One of the guides came over to our table and told us that a few people had dropped out, they had extra places and supplies, and would we like to go? What do you do when a wish is suddenly granted?

I asked when they were leaving, and he said, In about an hour, and I asked how long we had to decide, and he said, About half an hour. There were logistical questions: did we have all the gear we needed, could we leave the car, did we have a way to get back to it, would anyone miss us, could we hike out at Phantom Ranch halfway down, did we trust these people? We already knew we wanted to get into that river that had sung us asleep that night, to be carried away on the current into the deep folds of the earth, back through time to the creation. And so we went back to the river guide and shocked him by saying yes, we would go, for a week or two, on twenty minutes' notice. It was his turn to retreat and mull things over, and he returned to us a little while later saying that the rangers had said we were not on the insurance list and so they could not take us. So we thanked him and went onward on dry land.

That yes was a huge landmark in my life, a dividing point. I'd wrestled against the inner voice of my mother, the voice of

night. In paintings Cupid, the unknown lover, is often portrayed with the wings

caution, of duty, of fear of the unknown, the voice that said the world was dangerous and safety was always the first measure and that often confused pleasure with danger, the mother who had, when I'd moved to the city, sent me clippings about young women who were raped and murdered there, who elaborated on obscure perils and injuries that had never happened to her all her life, and who feared mistakes even when the consequences were minor. Why go to Paradise when the dishes aren't done? What if the dirty dishes clamor more loudly than Paradise?

She had an adventurous streak herself and had talked her younger sister into touring the country by bus when they were young, had moved to Florida alone rather than staying home with her mother as an unmarried girl of her day generally did, had married a Jew who immediately took her away to live in Germany during his military service and then took her to live in the far west and South America. She had turned down adventures too, and she had chosen many things for many years for safety and thrift, sacrificed the present for security in the imagined future again and again, and was wistful for many what-might-have-beens. She had said no too many times, out of fear, out of duty, and in all this I had been tutored.

When you say *mother* or *father* you describe three different phenomena. There is the giant who made you and loomed over your early years; there is whatever more human-scale version might have been possible to perceive later and maybe even befriend; and there is the internalized version of the parent with whom you struggle—to appease, to escape, to be yourself, to understand and be understood by—and they make up a chaotic and contradictory trinity. In saying yes to the river, I had overcome

of a bird, Psyche with those of a butterfly. Nevertheless it is he that is the moth,

some internalized version of my mother that had become almost a reflex of cautious duty.

I came out of that minor adventure with a motto that stood me in good stead ever after—"Never turn down an adventure without a really good reason"—that I used to assay any invitation or possibility I was about to reflexively dismiss. A dozen years or more after we had said yes, Sophie fell in love with a man on the other side of the country, decided early in the romance to quit her miserable job to go be with him, and was told by her parents in a letter that she was making a big mistake in this leap into the unknown, this abandonment of a reliable step on a secure career.

I drove her to the airport for the flight that would take her back to her love. On the drive we talked about the time we'd chosen the unknown. If we had said no, we would have always wondered what would have happened, we would have forever felt that we'd turned down a treasure that could have been ours, had turned down a chance to live—and what mattered is that we had said yes to adventure, to the unknown, to possibility. If she didn't go, I told Sophie, she'd always wonder about the man, and if she went and it did not work out, she would have tried and she would know, and if it did work out—.

I told a version of the river story at their wedding. They have two children now, the whirlwind is serene and has found her direction and her place, and of course her parents long ago forgot they had tried to stamp out her impulsive leap. I said yes to other adventures, and in that year of the apricots I was invited as abruptly and even more unexpectedly to Iceland, and I said yes instantly.

---

coming at night, feeding on her, ravishing her in the dark, laying low by day. The

---

3 · Ice

The expanse of smooth snow and jagged ice rising into small peaks and ranges seemed to go on forever, to dwarf the figures pursuing each other across it, and to threaten or promise to swallow them. They were small dark forms like two letters on an otherwise blank page, overwhelmed by that whiteness. They drew closer to each other as though to form a word that would never be sounded, drew apart into wordlessness and silence, but the landscape promised them a kind of immortality: the immortality of cold in which nothing decays.

It was a chase on film, or rather, on a grainy television, but it captivated me when I saw it in my early teens. It was my first vision of the arctic and the far north, and it launched a lasting desire to go there, to see the absolute, the uttermost, the far beyond, the end of the earth, the world whited out, the cold primordial forces of water, wind, cold, and spaciousness. It was the opening or the closing of one of the dozens of cinematic versions of Mary Shelley's *Frankenstein*.

The week before the apricots arrived, I'd been asked to write an essay about the far north for a museum show of several artists whose work was about that realm. The north organizes all modern maps and much of my sense of direction: to know where I am anywhere on this side of the equator I face north in body or imagination, like a magnetized needle. The needle points north, and

rest of the old tale is familiar. Urged into suspicion and curiosity by her jealous

so do I. In midsummer in my mild climate I thought of what I knew of the arctic and subarctic, of my long desire to go far north enough to live for a little while under the midnight sun, of that early vision of a world of ice, and of *Frankenstein*.

Most *Frankenstein* movies have run away with the idea of a mad scientist and a vengeful, lurching monster, far from the more sober, psychological novel, and few remember that the book begins and ends in the arctic, where Victor Frankenstein in pursuit of his creature and near death himself comes across a stranded ship, locked up in the ice. On that ship, in company with its stubborn, lonely, ambitious young captain, he is saved for a little while, and to that captain seeking the North Pole he tells his story.

The book is composed in the Russian-doll mode, for the beginning and end belong to the polar explorer, Robert Walton, and everything else is retrospect, told in the ship's cabin. We read in Captain Walton's letters to his sister first his own story, of seeking a paradise in the undiscovered north, and then what he heard from Frankenstein, who at one point tells Walton what he heard from the creature he brought to life. Thus, midway through the tale, the creature tells his creator the dramatic tale of a family he spied on and grew fond of, and theirs constitutes a story within a story within a story within the captain's story in this book framed by ice.

Ice and cold are principal emblems of the book. Walton himself imagines that he will discover a marvelous country, will discover the secret of why the magnetized needles of compasses point north, may discover the Northwest Passage that would speed trade, imagines that he will benefit mankind in his willful pursuit. He is torn between ambition and empathy, between

sisters, the girl with butterfly wings acquires a desire to see him. She lights a lamp

pursuing his goals to their uttermost end and saving his men's lives by turning back. When he encounters Frankenstein, his boat is "nearly surrounded by ice, which closed in the ship on all sides, scarcely leaving her the sea room in which she floated. About two o'clock the mist cleared away, and we beheld, stretched out in every direction, vast and irregular plains of ice, which seemed to have no end."

Ice the destroyer: cold slows things down. In freezing conditions, liquid becomes solid, and the flow and motion of even the inanimate largely stops, and, at the impossible temperature of absolute zero, atoms, molecules, entropy, would stop, and of course life would have ceased long before. Some simple animals freeze solid and then thaw, life stopped and then restarted, and creatures like polar bears and penguins have adaptations that allow them to swim in frigid waters and sleep on ice without harm, but most creatures are menaced by severe cold.

And ice the preserver: the long cores from Greenland's ice sheet whose air bubbles contain the atmosphere of bygone millennia, the frozen remains of the past found in the far north and the high peaks. Mountaineers who die at the highest levels remain there in perpetuity, stopped at the moment of their death, blanching and desiccating a little but not decaying. Robert Macfarlane tells the story of a European woman whose mountaineer father died high in the Himalayas when she was an infant. At twenty she came to see where he died and found that he had shifted out of his grave, so that she was able to look into his frozen, preserved face and cut a lock of his hair.

It's a realm of a certain kind of purity, unmuddled by life, by the activity of organisms that reproduce and decay, a nearly

in the darkness. It drips one burning drop of oil that scalds sleeping love with pain.

monochromatic world of white and blue and gray and black. Nothing decays in extreme cold. In 1991 the corpse of a man emerged from an Austrian-Italian glacier 5,300 years after his death, eroded and compressed, but intact down to his tattoos, weapons, and the contents of his last meals in his frozen stomach. Survivors of a deeper past, mammoths in Siberia, now appear more often in that frozen world now melting.

Cold preserves almost anything. The very word *freeze* is synonymous in modern English with stopping time, stopping progress, stopping a film, and if time is a river, then perhaps its water may turn to ice. This stopped and stalled time is the far north's obdurate stability. And then there is the dramatic instability of its coastlines as they annually freeze up and melt. The arrival of the ice landlocked coastal villages and froze ships in place until spring thaw, created fissures in the land, turned water into a solid that could be traveled across on foot and by sled. The melt turned that solid ice into an armada of crashing, disintegrating rafts on which people and animals might be stranded, as Frankenstein was when Walton plucked him off an ice floe.

When I was eighteen, I put a map of Antarctica on the wall of my room in the fleabag residential hotel that was my home. It represented a kind of cold hope beyond suffering and passion, beyond society and personality, beyond the familiar and ordinary, a landscape for extremists. That pure far world still fascinates me, that world north or south of trees, of cities, of almost everything, seemingly even of color in those images of white expanses through which white and drab animals move, under a pale or cloudy sky, the elemental earth, the other world at the ends of the world.

He reacts as if he never before knew pain, and perhaps he didn't, perhaps gods

---

Those in the temperate zone often think of the tropics as exuberant and profligate by comparison with the cautious, conservative north, but this is far from true in terms of how the arctic and antarctic regions consume their annual budget of light. The same amount of light and darkness falls on all parts of the earth, but not in the same measure. The equatorial zone portions out its annual budget of light so that days and nights are the same length, year-round. It is a sensible arrangement with little twilight or dawn and much sun directly overhead—a steady, reliable, static plan of light taken in even-size daily doses. And then there is the extravagance of places where summer hardly has darkness and winter hardly has light, as though the light were gambled away or drunk down all in one long exhilarated draught that brings on the long darkness.

Mary Shelley once wrote in her journal that her life with her poet husband was "more passing than an Italian twilight" and made this wish for their newfound tranquillity: "May it be a Polar day; yet that, too, has an end." A summer day at the Pole she must mean, prolonged into unbroken months of light. Part of the madness of Captain Walton in the novel is his description of the arctic as "the region of beauty and delight. There . . . the sun is for ever visible; its broad disk just skirting the horizon, and diffusing a perpetual splendor." He has described its nightless summer but not its dayless winter. That time itself is different there marks the strangeness of the north.

We use the language of temperature to describe character and emotion: warmhearted, cold shoulder, icy disposition, the heat of passion. Little more than a year after that entry about the polar sun, a few months after her husband's sudden death by drowning,

don't until some mortal violates the rules to look at them and burns them with

Mary Shelley herself wrote, "Have I a cold heart? God knows! But none need envy the icy region this heart encircles; and at least the tears are hot which the emotions of this cold heart forces me to shed." She had often been called cold because she was reserved.

A year before the summer during which she began *Frankenstein,* she had lost her first child, a baby girl born prematurely who lived two weeks and then died in the night, so calmly that Mary thought she was sleeping and did not try to wake her until morning. "I am no longer a mother now," she wrote a friend. On March 19, 1815, she had written in her journal: "Dream that my little baby came to life again—that it had only been cold & that we rubbed it before the fire & it lived. Awoke and found no baby. I think about the little thing all day." And then she dreamed of it again.

Warmth was life, but cold saved her once. A few years after the death of that first daughter, after the birth of three and death of two more children, when she nearly died from a miscarriage, far from any doctor, her husband, Percy Shelley, saved her by plunging her into a tub of ice and water and, apparently, slowing down the bleeding. Not long after, he plunged into seawater to die, going out in a sailboat with a storm approaching, leaving her a widow with one surviving child. Birth and death were never far apart in her life.

Frankenstein is often remarked upon as a novel in which a man usurps a woman's power of creating life, which serves as a roundabout reminder that in this way women may be gods and men not, but the man at the center of her novel makes this life out of dead things and elemental forces. He confesses, "I collected bones from charnel houses and with profane fingers meddled with the

the sorrow of their gaze, the sorrow that belongs to us and not to them. So often

secrets of the human frame." Just as Walton imagines himself as a benefactor of mankind even while he endangers the lives of the actual men with him, so Frankenstein imagines himself as a savior. But when he brings his creature to life and then flees it, he is both a parent abandoning a child and a citizen walking away from a calamity in the making. The coldness of this novel that begins and ends in the arctic and climaxes in the great glacial landscape of the high Alps is the coldness of his heart.

Mary Shelley was only eighteen when she began writing the novel and twenty when it was published. Some of its inspirations are well known. In 1815 a volcano, Mount Tambora, on an island in a Javanese archipelago that is now part of Indonesia, erupted. The most powerful eruption in more than 1,600 years, it killed thousands directly and tens or hundreds of thousands more through famine from the fallen ash and from the strange weather that followed. In Europe and North America, 1816 was known as the year without a summer.

Spring advanced as usual that year, and then it was as though the clock ran backward: the weather became colder instead of warmer, a dry fog covered the northeastern United States, so dimming the sun that sunspots could be seen with the naked eye, crops froze, withered, and failed, snow fell in June, there was ice on the water of lakes and rivers in July and August. In Italy the summer snow was red with ash from the volcano. There were famines. The cold itself was a sign of strangeness and disorder, a nature that had become unnatural and deadly. Mary was not of the class that starved, but she was in Switzerland where the food riots were the most intense in all Europe.

Fifteen years later she recalled, "It proved a wet, uncongenial

in these myths we hear how the human becomes divine, immortal, impervious,

summer, and incessant rain often confined us for days to the house. Some volumes of ghost stories, translated from the German into French, fell into our hands. I have not seen these stories since then; but their incidents are as fresh in my mind as if I had read them yesterday. 'We will each write a ghost story,' said Lord Byron; and his proposition was acceded to. There were four of us." The other three were the poet Byron, who didn't write a story but did write a nightmarish poem, "Darkness"; his friend Dr. Polidori, who drafted *The Vampyre,* the gothic tale that begat the immortal genre of vampire stories; and the poet Percy Bysshe Shelley, who didn't contribute to the project.

Two summers earlier, a few months before her seventeenth birthday, after those joint visits to her mother's grave, she had eloped with the poet. It was both the start of a great artistic alliance and a cliché from the novels of imperiled female virtue of the time: she was pretty and poor, and he was the reckless, willful, aristocratic heir to a title and a fortune. Shelley seems to have fallen in love a little with what she signified before he grasped who she was. She was a brilliant, strong-willed young woman who would be a fit intellectual companion to him, as well as an ardent, devoted partner, but to him she was first the daughter of the anarchist William Godwin and the feminist Mary Wollstonecraft.

Wollstonecraft had given birth once before without incident, but in giving birth to Mary Godwin Shelley contracted the infection that raged through her, ravaged her with extraordinary pain, and ended her life ten days after the birth. Her mother found death in birth; Mary Shelley herself entered the world as a killer, if an innocent, unwitting one, and lost all but one of the children she gave birth to. She launched her relationship with Shelley,

but there should be a story heading in the other direction, whereby a god becomes

maybe consummated it, on visits with him to her mother's grave in London's St. Pancras churchyard when she was sixteen. And then she wrote a novel that turns the story of her birth inside out, so that a man makes birth out of death.

Wollstonecraft had had her own adventures in the far north, and these too seem to have been an influence upon *Frankenstein*. She had gone to France to witness the French Revolution in 1792, fallen in love with a swindler, adventurer, and former soldier of the American Revolution, Gilbert Imlay, borne him a child, and been abandoned by him in quick succession. Wollstonecraft's letters show her to be ardent, devoted, badgering, self-pitying, and incapable of giving up on a romance that had been sour longer than it had been sweet, even when Imlay established himself in London with an actress mistress and otherwise spurned her.

Devastated and suicidal, though tenderly devoted to her daughter Fanny and eager to win back Imlay's love, Wollstonecraft set out for Scandinavia to locate his stolen merchant ship with its load of silver he'd had smuggled out of France, through the English naval blockade. It was a daring adventure, particularly for a woman with a small child (and French nursemaid) in tow, in remote lands where few spoke English. She confronted the dishonest captain in Norway and pursued the case with various authorities, but never recovered the silver or got recompense. What she brought back instead was a more precious load of observations, analyses, and emotions, first drafted in letters to Imlay, then recast as a travel narrative, *Letters Written During a Short Residence in Sweden, Norway, and Denmark*.

The slender volume mingled mournful personal expression and brief evocative descriptions of the terrain with headlong social

human, for love, because of pain. Love has been burned and made visible, and

and political critiques of the comparatively democratic, but to her eyes backward, cultures she encountered. Wollstonecraft spoke of death, of melancholy, of abandonment, of injustice, and more, taxing her distant lover with his sins again and again in letters that were better at establishing her neediness than winning him back. She made another suicide attempt when she returned, jumping into the Thames on a rainy night, only to be pulled out again. But her book was a great success.

The poet Robert Southey wrote of Wollstonecraft: "She has made me in love with a cold climate, and frost and snow, with a northern moonlight." She may have written the book to win back Imlay with a demonstration of her fine mind and strong feeling, but at this she failed. However, the middle-aged William Godwin wrote, "If ever there was a book calculated to make a man in love with its author, this appears to me to be the book." He did fall in love and begat upon her Mary Godwin Shelley, who is thereby, in some sense, the fruit of a match made by a book on northernness, distance, and grief.

Godwin liked married life enough to try it again after Wollstonecraft died of birth, this time with a vehement, unintellectual woman who brought two illegitimate children to the ménage of Godwin, his daughter, and his stepdaughter Fanny Imlay. A son, Mary's half-brother, was born when she was six. This household of two adults and five children, no two of whom had the same pair of parents, struggled on, her father writing children's books under an assumed name and working as a bookseller himself. Not quite a wicked stepmother, the new Mrs. Godwin was nevertheless unsympathetic and perhaps hostile. One of Mary's childhood memories was being dragged by this stepmother out from under

he flees. To regain her bird-winged love, Psyche must sort by evening a mountain

the parlor sofa where she had hidden to hear Samuel Taylor Coleridge recite his "Rime of the Ancient Mariner" in 1806, a decade before she began her novel.

That poem of sin, accursed wandering, and its memorable scenes of icebergs sailing by, calving and cracking, may be another of the major influences on her first novel, and wanderers and outcasts were fixtures in Romantic writing, from Wordsworth's displaced peasants to novels about the Wandering Jew. But despite the exotic settings, much of *Frankenstein* seems to be made direct out of the material of Mary's own life, even as Frankenstein's creature is made out of human remains. Her father had once advocated free love but cut off Mary when she ran off with Shelley. This parent who disowns a child is one version of the irresponsible, distancing inventor that is her Victor Frankenstein.

And Shelley himself is another. Frankenstein is likewise a firstborn son, likewise educated in old alchemical and magical branches and new electrical and medical branches of science. Shelley's willfulness, his pursuit of his destiny and his pleasures no matter the cost to others, is also an attribute of Frankenstein, who again and again distances himself from the family he claims to love. Early in the book, her protagonist himself proclaims that no man should allow his pursuit to "interfere with his tranquility and his domestic affections," and similar arguments crop up elsewhere in the book. But Frankenstein shatters those things and travels far in lonely pursuit of his aims.

Young, poor, and female in an age where women had almost no power, Mary assumed the status of an omniscient giant in her book, describing the world on her own terms, depicting her own vision of a world gone wrong, and writing a masterpiece that

of several kinds of grains and beans mixed together, an impossible task until a

would dwarf all the works of the Romantic poets in the directness of its impact on the collective imagination. The cinematic version has become so familiar that "Frankenstein" has become the oft-invoked byword for reckless, irresponsible science, and the template for a thousand imitations. It is the rare story that becomes, like a myth or fairy tale, part of the necessary furnishings of the imagination and shorthand for an aspect of the human condition. It is the progenitor of a whole genre of books and movies with mad scientists and has inspired the occasional masterpiece, such as the exquisitely melancholy Spanish film *The Spirit of the Beehive.*

In that burst of inspiration in the wintry summer of 1816, Mary Shelley drew ideas from the conversations of Byron and Shelley about the principles of life, electricity, and other developing scientific matters; from the horror stories they were all telling and reading and the macabre often invoked by Shelley; from a certain spirit of fearless ambition, and the milieu seems to have supercharged her. Certainly, she never again wrote anything so close to a myth in its power. But it is still her own creation, her immortal child. Frankenstein assembles a superhumanly powerful abomination but she composed an undying work of art.

In bringing the creature to life, the medical student becomes three things that echo one another: a parent, an artist, and a god; three kinds of makers. The responsibility of the creator to his creation is the overarching question in this book that is sometimes also about our responsibility to each other, about the empathy and engagement that might prevent such solitary experimenting, such willful individualism. It's a conservative book at heart, not in favor of conventional mores but of the ties of obligation and affection

throng of ants carries out the work on her behalf. A reed, an eagle, and a tower

over individual pursuits, and in that too is a veiled reproach of her husband, the willful, restless, and often selfish poet.

Frankenstein brought fascination and dedication to the making of the creature and little forethought to its actual existence. He made it; he was frightened and repulsed; he ran. His moral weakness, his irresponsibility, is what sets everything in motion, that and the deeply human emotions of the creature who wants fellowship, love, and understanding, and receives rejection. That hideous creature is all too human and particularly adolescent, with an adolescent's furious sense of justice. The novel prefigures not only debates about scientific responsibility, but also liberal arguments that blame environment and upbringing for bad behavior. "I am malicious because I am miserable. You, my creator, would tear me to pieces and triumph," says the creature, blaming his parent for his crimes.

Loneliness is his justification for killing, and had the doctor met his creation with compassion, they might yet both have been redeemed. They go on instead at odds with each other, the creature inflicting misery on him by proxy with its murders. After he murders Frankenstein's bride on her wedding night, the tables turn and the creator hunts his creation across the north by sledge until he ends up in Walton's ship, dying. He represents artists, makers, parents, and gods, but also something more essential, the self and its limits, for at a deeper level the monster is not his creation so much as it is the self he will not face, not own, not know.

Two novels at the other end of the nineteenth century, *The Strange Case of Dr. Jekyll and Mr. Hyde* and *The Picture of Dorian Gray,* make explicit the idea of another, monstrous self hidden

help her with subsequent endeavors: the whole overlooked, voiceless world speaks

from itself and from others. Both writers make beauty, the beauty that makes others empathize, and its opposite, repulsion, forces in their novels. The ugliness of Mr. Hyde is testament to his criminality—he is Dr. Jekyll's own dark side separated and let loose—but Dorian Gray sells his soul for a beauty that remains unchanged by his crimes and his coldness, until the end, when his decaying portrait and corporeal self change roles. Wilde is more distrustful of beauty.

Not to know yourself is dangerous, to that self and to others. Those who destroy, who cause great suffering, kill off some portion of themselves first, or hide from the knowledge of their acts and from their own emotion, and their internal landscape fills with partitions, caves, minefields, blank spots, pit traps, and more, a landscape turned against itself, a landscape that does not know itself, a landscape through which they may not travel. You see the not-knowing in wars in which the reality of death, the warm, messy, excruciating dismemberment of bodies, the blood and the screams, and the unbearable bereavement of survivors, is abstracted into collateral damage or statistics or overlooked altogether, or in which the enemy is recategorized as nonhuman.

You see it too in the small acts of everyday life, of the person who feels perfectly justified, of the person who doesn't know he's just committed harm, of the person who says something whose motives are clear to everyone but her, of the person who comes up with intricate rationales or just remains oblivious, of the person we've all been at one time or another. Taken to an extreme, it's the mind-set of murder; enlarged in scale it's war. Elaborate are the means to hide from yourself, the disassociations, projections, deceptions, forgettings, justifications, and other tools to detour

with her and seems to be on her side. The tale of Cupid and Psyche is told by an

around the obstruction of unbearable reality, the labyrinths in which we hide the minotaurs who have our faces. Walton imagines a north pole where it is perpetually light, eternally summer; he hides from the darkness and the rest of the year, as Frankenstein hides from that part of himself that looks like a monster. Accident and abuse make destructive people in civilian life; the military makes them intentionally, through training procedures that make killing automatic, reflexive, and the enemy unreal.

Many of the great humanitarian and environmental campaigns of our time have been to make the unknown real, the invisible visible, to bring the faraway near, so that the suffering of sweatshop workers, torture victims, beaten children, even the destruction of other species and remote places, impinges on the imagination and perhaps prompts you to act. It's also a narrative art of explaining the connections between your food or your clothing or your government and this suffering far from sight in which you nonetheless play a role. The suffering before you, in your own home or bed or life, can be harder to see, sometimes, as is the self who is implicated.

The self is also a creation, the principal work of your life, the crafting of which makes everyone an artist. This unfinished work of becoming ends only when you do, if then, and the consequences live on. We make ourselves and in so doing are the gods of the small universe of self and the large world of repercussions. If *Frankenstein* is to be thought of as a fairy tale, it would be the tale of Walton, who in the midst of his folly rescues a dying stranger, or is rescued by that stranger's tale. He learns from Frankenstein's mistakes of vainglorious isolation and prepares to turn back from his pursuit of polar death and glory, toward the temperate world,

old woman held captive by thieves in The Golden Ass, *a novel written in Latin*

fellowship, and survival. The brief tale of Walton wraps all around Frankenstein's story like an outer shell, and around the whole book hovers the tale of Mary Shelley.

In the years she gave birth to all those too-mortal children, she also created a work of art that yet lives, a monster of sorts in its depth of horror, and a beauty in the strength of its vision and its acuity in describing the modern world that in 1816 was just emerging. This is the strange life of books that you enter alone as a writer, mapping an unknown territory that arises as you travel. If you succeed in the voyage, others enter after, one at a time, also alone, but in communion with your imagination, traversing your route. Books are solitudes in which we meet.

about A.D. 160 by the North African Apuleius. Like the Arabian Nights, it

4 · Flight

Many stories are told about the T'ang Dynasty artist Wu Daozi, sometimes named as one of the three great sages of China: that he ignored color and only painted in black ink; that he transgressively painted his own face on an image of the Buddha; that he painted a perfect halo in a single stroke without the aid of compasses; that he painted pictures of the dragons who cause rain so well that the paintings themselves exuded water; that the emperor sent him to sketch a beautiful region and reprimanded him for coming back empty-handed, after which he painted a hundred-foot scroll that replicated all his travels in one continuous flow; that he made all his paintings boldly and without hesitation, painting like a whirlwind, so that people loved to watch the world emerge from under his brush.

One story about him I read long ago I have always remembered. While he was showing the emperor the landscape he had painted on a wall of the Imperial Palace, he pointed out a grotto or cave, stepped into it, and vanished. Some say that the painting disappeared too. In the account I remember, he was a prisoner of the emperor and escaped through his painting. When I was much younger, I saw another version of this feat that impressed me equally.

In an episode of the Road Runner and Coyote cartoon, the eternally hopeful predator makes a trap for the bird. At the point

contains tales within tales. Though the old woman "bent with age" is poor and

where a road ends in a precipice, he places a canvas on which he paints an extension of the road, complete with the red cliff on one side and the guardrail on the other. The Road Runner neither smashes into the painting nor falls through it, but runs into it and vanishes around the painted bend. When the coyote attempts to follow him, he breaks through the painting, plummets, is smashed up, and then, yet again, as always, he is resurrected. Your door is my wall; your wall is my door.

The one creature embodies grace, the other foolish desire, as though they are two elemental principles that can never mingle, in body or spirit. Chuck Jones's Wile E. Coyote is a version of the great creator deity of the North American continent, Coyote. This is the god whose eyes and cock sometimes detach to seek their own satisfactions, who is often broken, occasionally killed, always resurrected, and never annihilated, who represents the comic principle of survival. But only as I write do I also notice the bird is a Taoist master, like the calm masters nothing could touch in the stories of old China. They walked through fire, through rock, and on air with aplomb.

These feats of the bird and the painter are paradoxical and impossible, but only literally, or only in some media. People disappear into their stories all the time. We live in stories and images, as immersed in them as though they were Wu Daozi's inkpots; we breathe in presuppositions and exhale further stories. We in the West have been muddled by Plato's assertion that art is imitation and illusion; we believe that it is a realm apart, one whose impact on our world is limited, one in which we do not live.

Sticks and stones may break my bones but words will never hurt me, my mother liked to recite, though words hurt her all the

abject, the tale she tells is of princesses and gods, one of the great allegories of love

time, and behind the words the stories about how things should be and where she fell short, as told by my father, by society, by the church, by the happy flawless women of advertisements. We all live in that world of images and stories, and most of us are damaged by some version of it, and if we're lucky, find others or make better ones that embrace and bless us.

As I wrote this my friend Annie sent me a note from Easter Island, where she was working on a radio story. She wrote me of "sweeping grasslands, dormant volcanoes, sheer black volcanic cliffs dropping into the sea and those magnificent, stern moai"—the great stone heads—"scattered all over the island. I can't stop wondering what possessed the Rapa Nui to build them and then after that was over to conceive of the birdman cult." Hundreds of years after the cultural near-extinction of their makers, the heads were still provoking thought; they were still in our heads; Annie wrote to me and put the birdman cult in mine.

After their devastating contact with the European world, beginning on Easter of 1722, the Rapa Nui, the Easter Island people, made the cult with its dangers and arbitrarinesses more central to their lives. Those who had the gift of prophesy would choose the contestants in their dreams. To be dreamed of was a dangerous thing. The contestants would swim to an islet off the coast, attempt to collect the first sooty tern egg of the season, swim back, then scale a cliff without breaking the egg. The losers sometimes drowned, or were devoured by sharks, or fell from the cliff. The winner was given a new name and isolated but exalted status for the year, and his clan won exclusive rights to the season's egg gathering from the small island where the tern's egg had been seized.

and the evolution of the soul. You can read "Cupid and Psyche" as a romance in

The birdman cult might be just an extreme case of the stories we weave all the time that make a small item a trophy, a sign of spiritual or social status, a token that changes your life. Only the unfamiliarity of the birdman cult makes us remark on its arbitrariness, since in our society people die in the attempt to climb mountains for no practical reason, kill because of words that insult them or their gods, and revere those who have won a prize handed out by a whimsical jury or because a combination of factors sent a ball into or over a net.

We live in dreams; we go into the shark-filled sea to carry them out; we make one egg of the sooty tern, also known as the wide-awake, into something to organize a whole society around. The tern's egg is small, speckled, nondescript. The god who presided over all this was named MakeMake. "The things we dream up . . ." wrote Annie. To become a maker is to make the world for others, not only the material world but the world of ideas that rules over the material world, the dreams we dream and inhabit together.

Like many others who turned into writers, I disappeared into books when I was very young, disappeared into them like someone running into the woods. What surprised and still surprises me is that there was another side to the forest of stories and the solitude, that I came out that other side and met people there. Writers are solitaries by vocation and necessity. I sometimes think the test is not so much talent, which is not as rare as people think, but purpose or vocation, which manifests in part as the ability to endure a lot of solitude and keep working. Before writers are writers they are readers, living in books, through books, in the lives of

a literal sense, or as the attempt of consciousness and desire to reconcile, to find a

others that are also the heads of others, in that act that is so intimate and yet so alone.

These vanishing acts are a staple of children's books, which often tell of adventures that are magical because they travel between levels and kinds of reality, and the crossing over is often an initiation into power and into responsibility. They are in a sense allegories first for the act of reading, of entering an imaginary world, and then of the way that the world we actually inhabit is made up of stories, images, collective beliefs, all the immaterial appurtenances we call ideology and culture, the pictures we wander in and out of all the time. In children's books there are inanimate objects that come to life, speaking statues, rings and words of power, talismans and amulets, and most of all, there are doors, particularly in the series that I, like so many children, took up imaginative residence in for some years, the Chronicles of Narnia.

I read one in fourth grade after a teacher who barely knew me handed it to me in the school library; I can still picture his mustache and the wall of books. I read it and read it again and then began to save up to buy the seven books, one at a time. The paperbacks came from the enchanted bookstore in the middle of town, whose kind proprietor rewarded me with the case in which the seven books fit when I had paid for the last one. I still have the boxed set, a little tattered, though I think no one has ever read them other than me. When I took one out recently, I noticed how dirty the white back of the book was from my small filthy fingers then.

Much has been written about the Christian themes, British boarding-school mores, and other contentious aspects of the series,

way to coexist. Read this way they are not two beings but two aspects of a being.

but little has been said about its doors. There is of course the wardrobe in the first book C. S. Lewis wrote, the wardrobe made of wood cut from an apple tree grown from seeds from another world that, when the four children walk into it, sometimes opens onto that world. Two of the other books feature a doorway that stands alone so that when you walk around it, it is just a frame, three pieces of wood in a landscape, but when you step through it, it leads to another world. There's a painting of a boat that comes to life as the children tumble over the picture frame into the sea and another world. There are books and maps that come to life as you look at them.

And there is the Wood Between the Worlds in the book *The Magician's Nephew,* which tells the creation story for Narnia, a wood described so enchantingly I sometimes think of it as a vision of peace still. It's more serene and more strange than the rest of the books with their busy symbolism—talking beasts, dwarves, witches, battles, enchantments, castles, and more. The young protagonist puts on a ring and finds himself coming up through a pool to the forest.

"It was the quietest wood you could possibly imagine. There were no birds, no insects, no animals, and no wind. You could almost feel the trees growing. The pool he had just got out of was not the only pool. There were dozens of others—a pool every few yards as far as his eyes could reach. You could almost feel the trees drinking the water up with their roots. This wood was very much alive." It is the place where nothing happens, the place of perfect peace; it is itself not another world but an unending expanse of trees and small ponds, each pond like a looking glass you can go

After Psyche's tasks are completed and the lovers are reunited, she gives birth to

through to another world. It is a portrait of a library, just as all the magic portals are allegories for works of art, across whose threshold we all step into other worlds.

Libraries are sanctuaries from the world and command centers onto it: here in quiet rooms are the lives of Crazy Horse and Aung San Suu Kyi, the Hundred Years' War and the Opium Wars and the Dirty War, the ideas of Simone Weil and Lao-tzu, information on building your sailboat or dissolving your marriage, fictional worlds and books to equip the reader to reenter the real world. They are, ideally, places where nothing happens and where everything that has happened is stored up to be remembered and relived, the place where the world is folded up into boxes of paper. Every book is a door that opens onto another world, which might be the magic that all those children's books were alluding to, and a library is a Milky Way of worlds. All readers are Wu Daozi; all imaginative, engrossing books are landscapes into which readers vanish.

The object we call a book is not the real book, but its seed or potential, like a music score. It exists fully only in the act of being read; and its real home is inside the head of the reader, where the seed germinates, the symphony resounds. A book is a heart that only beats in the chest of another. The child I once was read constantly and hardly spoke, because she was ambivalent about the merits of communication, about the risks of being mocked or punished or exposed. The idea of being understood and encouraged, of recognizing herself in another, of affirmation, had hardly occurred to her and neither had the idea that she had something to give others. So she read, taking in words in huge quantities, a

immortal pleasure. Moths drink the tears of sleeping birds, and love like that of

children's and then an adult's novel a day for many years, seven books a week or so, gorging on books, fasting on speech, carrying piles of books home from the library.

Writing is saying to no one and to everyone the things it is not possible to say to someone. Or rather writing is saying to the no one who may eventually be the reader those things one has no someone to whom to say them. Matters that are so subtle, so personal, so obscure, that I ordinarily can't imagine saying them to the people to whom I'm closest. Every once in a while I try to say them aloud and find that what turns to mush in my mouth or falls short of their ears can be written down for total strangers. Said to total strangers in the silence of writing that is recuperated and heard in the solitude of reading. Is it the shared solitude of writing, is it that separately we all reside in a place deeper than society, even the society of two? Is it that the tongue fails where the fingers succeed, in telling truths so lengthy and nuanced that they are almost impossible aloud?

I started out in silence, writing as quietly as I had read, and then eventually people read some of what I had written, and some of the readers entered my world or drew me into theirs. I started out in silence and traveled until I arrived at a voice that was heard far away—first the silent voice that can only be read, and then I was asked to speak aloud and to read aloud. When I began to read aloud, another voice, one I hardly recognized, emerged from my mouth. Maybe it was more relaxed, because writing is speaking to no one, and even when you're reading to a crowd, you're still in that conversation with the absent, the faraway, the not yet born, the unknown, and the long gone for whom writers write, the crowd of the absent who hover all around the desk.

Cupid and Psyche is only one kind of symbiosis. Some species of yucca plant and

Sometime in the late nineteenth century, a poor rural English girl who would grow up to become a writer was told by a gypsy: "You will be loved by people you've never met." This is the odd compact with strangers who will lose themselves in your words and the partial recompense for the solitude that makes writers and writing. You have an intimacy with the faraway and distance from the near at hand. Like digging a hole to China and actually coming out the other side, the depth of that solitude of reading and then writing took me all the way through to connect with people again in an unexpected way. It was astonishing wealth for one who had once been so poor.

My own story in its particulars hardly interests me now. The incidents have dissolved into the dirt from which certain plants grew, and the blooms of those plants or maybe only their perfume on the air, the questions and ideas that arose, are what still signifies. Or so I think, but maybe a moment in the dirt of that apricot summer is necessary. The apricots arrived in early August, and then everything with my mother began to deteriorate more ferociously.

The place she was living was not working, the people who were supposed to advise us were not helping, and the three of us were worn out from the constant attendance, constant anxiety, and lack of any good ideas about what to do next. We took her on long walks every morning in hope of sating her restlessness. When it was my turn, we walked around the pleasant stucco and wooden houses surrounding her residence while I remarked on colors, on porches, on gables and bay windows, on morning glories, lilies, and sunflowers, and hollyhocks and foxglove.

Early in September she stepped out of a second-floor window

of moth depend upon each other. The white moths hatch out of their cocoons as

onto the first-floor roof of the careless care facility where she was living, because she imagined that she was a prisoner making a break for it. The window had been open for some workmen doing repairs, and she menaced them as they tried to keep her from the edge and get her back in. The next day she bolted through the front door after a brief scuffle, one of several violent moments in that poorly regulated place. She disappeared for a day during which the police in that town had an all-points bulletin out for her. If nothing else, she was proving to be in excellent physical health.

My brothers were out of town so I dropped everything and drove over to monitor the situation and see what I could do. I went to the main library where my friend worked in case she showed up there and found a picture of her already posted on the front door. Anything might've happened; she could have been hit by a car, fallen in with some of the bands of street people, gotten seriously lost, gone on one of the several-mile walks that had ended with her being returned by the police. When my younger brother arrived late that afternoon, he figured out that she'd managed to hitchhike and take buses and show up back at her old house twenty miles away, like one of those animals in the stories of faithful return. It was wrenching.

What she wanted was not what she needed. She'd forgotten the thousand fearful crises of her last few years in her house, ignored the fact that she could no longer make a meal on her own or keep track of a key, and spoke of life in that shuttered gray-green bungalow as a golden age that might just have been remembering life before the crises of her brain disease. The house was still hers but there was no going back from the disorder. We were

the white flowers open. They mate and the female pollinates the flowers while

told to find a new place for her promptly and to hire full-time one-on-one caregivers in the meantime, and so came a succession of blue-collar women of color of varying calibers of kindness and competence, along with huge bills from their agency. Choosing her medications was left up to me. I put her on an antidepressant and then when the trouble didn't cease, around the time of the incident on the roof and the running away, shortly after she broke the plate-glass door, added an anti-psychotic sometimes used for Alzheimer's agitation and violence.

I think my last lengthy conversation with the man I was involved with then was about choosing the drugs. The crises with my mother had burdened the relationship, but the relationship had burdened everything else too. It was in trouble for various reasons, but everything had been becalmed for a few years because of my crises with my mother's health and his or ours with his own. He'd been suddenly struck down by a disorder that inflicted constant disabling pain, that turned him from a long-distance runner into someone who walked as though on coals or across thorns. For the two years before the apricot summer I was sandwiched between two severely sick people whose needs flattened mine, and though it was clear that little or nothing could be asked of my mother it was unclear what could be asked of him.

He cited his pain as an excuse for everything, which it wasn't, but the pain was real. He broke up with me by phone a week after the peak of the crises with my mother, and I was furious that he was not there for me after I had gotten him through so many of his crises. Then he changed his mind, but there was too much damage to restore, and I was too busy coping with my mother's emergency. The particulars don't matter now. There was bitterness but also

laying her eggs in them, so that they will produce the fruit on which her offspring

relief that I was no longer responsible for trying to get him to make better decisions about his life and mine.

A young man who was transcribing the interviews for the book I was working on turned out to have a mother who was a great expert on Alzheimer's and a kind woman. She advised me about our mother's condition in the moment and as it might progress, and recommended the Alzheimer's residence in which she'd placed her own father, praising it as the best place in the region. I called. We visited. They had openings. A week after the revelations from the man in pain, I was walking my mother around the lake in the city where the residence was, hoping to put her in the best frame of mind for the intake interview, when my phone rang.

The call was from Reykjavík, and the caller invited me to come to Iceland. I startled her by replying yes without hesitation. At that moment, Iceland, the remote unknown, the back of the north wind, sounded like the right place to go, and the call came like a magical rescue, the most unlikely intervention at the most grueling moment.

The things that make our lives are so tenuous, so unlikely, that we barely come into being, barely meet the people we're meant to love, barely find our way in the woods, barely survive catastrophe every day. Your origin is due to two people come together, by accident, whether wisely or not, by the attractions of similarity and difference, who survive each other's fears and limits long enough to create the collision of the two cells from which you spring. A million sperm swim at every egg, and somehow the one that makes the journey all the way begets you in combination with that single maternal cell; the faintest rearrangement of that

will feed. The yucca survives only by the pollination efforts of this moth, the

unthinkable coupling and someone else arrives on earth out of that maze inside your mother; or no one comes into being; or your mother neglects one moment in that terrifying vulnerability that is your first few years and you are snuffed out like a candle, drowned in the bath, choked on a button found on the floor.

Everyone has stories of the small coincidence by which their parents met or their grandmother was saved from fire or their grandfather from the grenade, of the choice made by the most whimsical means that led to everything else, whether you're blessed or cursed or both. Trace it far enough and this very moment in your life becomes a rare species, the result of a strange evolution, a butterfly that should already be extinct and survives by the inexplicabilities we call coincidence. The word is often used to mean the accidental but literally means to fall together. The patterns of our lives come from those things that do not drift apart but move together for a little while, like dancers. They come together in those moments that are the coupling of unseen forces, a generative warmth, a secret romance between the unknowns that are also our parents.

The deus ex machina, the gods in machines used by ancient Greek playwrights to move the plot along or rescue a character, were not well regarded. The ancient critics felt that events should unfold from the acts and character of the central figures, not from outside forces. Perhaps there are people whose lives are as contained as a classical drama, in which the number of characters is set and finite, and nothing much wanders in to augment, disrupt, or rescue, but that's usually just a formal convention, a literary rule. Trace the lineage of any significant event, and coincidences and strangers appear from beyond the horizon of the calculable,

larvae survive only by consuming this particular fruit. They would not exist

from out of the blue. The other evening my friend Carolina told me about a bull that escaped from a bullfighting arena in her native Bogotá, ran down the street, and, frightened by the urban chaos, dashed into an elevator, where he gored the man within to death.

Whether the man was at the height of his happiness, desperate for life to change, or just persevering day by day, the bull interrupted all that. Every day some bull gets on the elevator; or a shark eats the other person trying to bring back the first sooty tern egg; or the phone rings and invites you to jump ship for the unknown. The innumerable gods have all sorts of machines at their disposal. Illness is one, and a sudden onset of serious illness changes the landscape profoundly, and not because of character or fate, unless that fate includes postclassical details like genetic predisposition or the odysseys of viruses.

As a young man, Saint Francis turned back from a military adventure because of malaria, and while convalescing settled into his spiritual destiny. A mosquito had spiritual consequence. The dirty hands of the doctor who attended Mary Wollstonecraft probably imparted the puerperal fever that killed her and left her newborn daughter to a cold fate. The gods in machines are just outside forces, and they are only outside the tight knot of fate and character that classical drama deems its only ingredients. Pull back, see farther, and they are inside the patterns of which our lives are made. They are bulls, are terns, are mosquitoes, are germs, among the myriad forms.

Two years later when the women who brought me to Iceland were sitting with me in my kitchen eating apricot halves from that harvest direct from the jar, I came to understand how I'd gotten

without each other, and yuccas of these species grown elsewhere have to be

there. The invitation came at that difficult moment like a key thrown into a prison, a raft in a shipwreck. But in a sense I made the raft myself, and the gods turned it into their machine. I sailed to Iceland on a raft made out of a book I had written. I had been sailing away on books all my life and in my childhood had built walls and towers of books all around me to protect myself from an unfriendly world.

That people were walking out of my books and pulling me into their world was a recent development. My story intersected with the story of a young man I never met, a man who was dying as I was embarked upon my crises, but whose life would not be entirely over, because the consequences of his acts, a stone thrown in others' waters, would ripple out for years, for lifetimes. He's here with you now in some way, because without him this book would not exist.

Once upon a time there was a wolf, or a young man of that name, Úlfur, which means wolf in Icelandic, a very Icelandic young man, though his father was African American. The young wolf was stricken with leukemia when he reached adulthood. Neither the hero nor the villain of this tale, he is instead the match to the tinder, though his own flame was almost out and his own story of which I know so little must be worth telling at greater length.

He had been the first love of a young Icelandic woman named Elín, and then they parted ways but stayed close. She went on to become an artist who made installations of sounds and shadows and small nuances and large environments, experiments in the phenomena and pleasures of the perceived world. He came to see her in her new home in Berlin for what turned out to be their last

---

hand-pollinated. Not all meals for moths are so exquisite or particular. A lot of

time together, on his way to treatment in Sweden, the kind of treatment that is a last resort, that can kill you or save you.

We associate skeletons with death, but bones generate life, abundantly, prolifically. The femurs, the ribs, the sternum, and other bones we see dry and white after death, in life harbor the marrow that produces billions of new blood cells daily, a bright red river gushing forth from bone. The process is called "hematopoiesis," from the ancient Greek words for blood and for making. Poetry comes from the same word, *poiesis,* and it belies Plato's argument that art is only imitation. Our word for poetry is their word for all the making in the world, of chairs, of houses, of bombs, of books, of blood, of gods. Making a poem is like making a chair; a poem is as real as a chair and sometimes more useful.

The young man kept making, made music, worked on films, loved, was loved back, struggled, traveled, endured for a while. About a quarter million people a year are diagnosed with leukemia, the disease that impairs or alters the making of the blood. I did not know the young wolf who died of it, and I did not know of his existence until after I went to Iceland, but he became a key that unlocked a door of my life, and perhaps I an extension of his; and I'm grateful.

Úlfur and Elín, during the rendezvous in Berlin, went to a bookstore—he had a talent for choosing books, said Elín and her mother long after at my kitchen table—and they picked out a book because its title seemed so relevant to their uncertain fate. It was one of mine. Then he went north for his bone marrow transplant and then home to Iceland. The operation did not work. He did not die immediately but they never saw each other again,

butterflies and moths engage in what is called "puddling," landing on pools of

because when he commenced to die she was too far away and he went too fast.

She drank the book down in one long gulp and marked it up, though she was not a reader generally. Like a lot of visual artists, she mostly plunged into the difficult books through which you hack your way slowly. She gave the book the wolf chose to her mother, and her mother kept it for several months and then read it on the airplane to my city to which she had never been before, to see the opening of the exhibition of her friend Olafur Eliasson. Olafur too had read a book of mine and sought me out when he came to install his prisms and crystals and tunnels and lights and shades and images of Iceland in a museum in my city.

That summer, while everything else was falling apart, the far north came calling. I had been commissioned to write about the north, had begun rereading *Frankenstein* and Barry Lopez's *Arctic Dreams,* and then this Icelandic man showed up trailing images and aspects of his country. I went many times to look at his tall wall of fragrant, thick Icelandic moss that gradually faded from green to pale yellow, his mirrored rooms, his big grids of photographs of Iceland, of islands in one grid, of horizons in another, his chamber of models of smaller crystals and faceted constructions, rooms of lights and shadows, a dark room of mist with rainbows glinting in it, an elemental world, an Icelandic world that was also the world of poesis, of making.

Olafur and Úlfur, Fríða and Elín, four people from a place I had never been to, a place I'd seen mostly in the pictures of a photographer I'd been commissioned to write about a dozen years earlier, whose images showed old sod houses melting back into a

water, piles of manure, rotting fruit, to feed. Moths of the genus Calyptra,

green landscape, threads of water streaming across black lava moss on stones, purity, and remoteness. Fríða landed in my town, went to her hotel, put on a black dress, and walked over to the opening reception for Olafur's show.

I came to it too, walked up and said hello to Olafur just as Fríða arrived, so he introduced us and we fell to talking as he was taken up by other obligations. She was my age and my height and not far from my coloring, though she was leaner and more glamorous, with cheekbones you could build castles on and magnificent poise. And so we met and I said it was a pity that she was just in town so briefly and offered to show her the city, prompted by some affinity or resemblance or maybe by her foreignness and by hospitality, since she was in my realm I knew and loved so well. It didn't hurt that she'd just finished my book. I also had a minor notion that someday it might be good to know someone in Iceland well enough to look them up for coffee, and Olafur had treated me with a courtesy that was a balm in those bad days.

I picked Fríða up the next morning and showed her facets of my city on the way to the airport as we talked about art, about books, about our parents with dementia, about light and seasons and weather. I told her that I'd always wanted to visit Iceland, but thought nothing of it until the other end of the month, when I was walking my mother around that lake, and the phone rang and Fríða asked if I'd like to be the first international resident at the Library of Water in Iceland, and I said yes.

Never turn down an invitation without a good reason, and I had every reason to seize this one with both hands. It was as though the book had become a door; people were entering the book and then stepping into my life and drawing me into theirs.

sometimes known as vampire moths, feed on vertebrate blood, and a dozen or

And it was my ticket out of deep trouble. Iceland would for the seven months it took me to actually get there serve as an amulet, a window onto another world, a thought that there was some place far away from all my troubles, and that I would myself be far away from them there soon enough.

There was even a webcam on the roof of the Library of Water I would log on to sometimes, with a view of the other world that would relieve me of this one. It showed a harbor near a great rock to which a causeway had been built, the town of square separate buildings like children's blocks, and beyond it the fjord full of islands and a sky sometimes full of clouds, sometimes of darkness. I watched it as snow arrived, as the days grew short and the webcam mostly showed harbor lights shining in blackness and headlights sweeping across snow. It was like a snow globe on my desk to shake in idle moments, but the world in it was real and awaited me. Like Wu Daozi I was going to step into the picture, through a door I had made myself, out of words.

more species of moth visit the eyes of mammals to drink fluids that provide

5 · Breath

A sentence by the Marquis de Sade I read when I was young sometimes returns to me: "Ah, what does it matter to her hand, which is always at work creating, that this or that mass of flesh which today constitutes an individual biped may be reproduced tomorrow in the form of a thousand insects?" It matters to the individual biped, but the exclamation in the form of a question points out that what is ordinarily imagined as disintegration is also, or instead, metamorphosis.

Even decay is a form of transformation into other living things, part of the great rampage of becoming that is also unbecoming. It is cruel, it is death, and it is also life, degeneration and regeneration, for nearly all things live by the death of other things. Even a harvest of wheat annihilates mice and insects unless poisons have sterilized the field beforehand; even the large animals we call herbivorous eat the small creatures on the grass as they graze. Even the earth and the very grass that grows out of that earth are carnivorous. The Marquis de Sade spoke with scorn for fear and attachment; the Zen teacher Shunryu Suzuki-Roshi was once asked by a sheepish student if he could sum up Zen in a sentence, and gave another version of the same answer: "Everything changes."

All stories are really fragments of one story, the metamorphoses, a fate sometimes as eagerly embraced as Daphne turning into

proteins, salts, and other minerals. Mostly males drink from these sources, and

a laurel tree to escape Apollo's embrace, sometimes resisted as frantically as the affluent arranging for their remains to be cryogenically frozen, but embracing or resisting are optional, and metamorphosis inevitable. You can rescue someone from danger, but not from change and death; the soldier who survives the battle becomes someone else, something else, somewhere else. His war subsides; his memory fades; his nation ceases to exist; all but the elemental structures decay away; the very atoms that were once warring sides are now soil, trees, lovers, birds; all the medals are playthings for strangers; the cannons have been melted down and turned back into church bells that will become cannons again for another war.

Have they been decaying for the length of four chapters, that horde or hoard of apricots on my bedroom floor, or only for the four or five days it took to do something about them? I culled the decaying fruits until my friend found a free evening, and we began to address the fruit together. It constituted a race against time, and time was winning. Time always wins; our victories are only delays; but delays are sweet, and a delay can last a whole lifetime.

For this mountain of stone fruit, though, not much more delay was possible. My apricots were being eaten by what I later read up on and found was brown rot, a common fruit fungus that arrives even on blossoms, though immature fruit generally resists it, unless that fruit suffers hail damage, insect feeding, or another injury. Ripe fruit is far more susceptible, and the fungus can appear as soft spots whose brown spreads rapidly. Some fruit undergoes a process that turns it into a wrinkled mummy, though my apricots seemed to head straight to soft brown mush, their

their meals give them resources for the spermatophores they provide to the females

liquid released as their cell walls broke down. Rot suggests something decaying, but the process is as much about something growing, something digesting its immediate surroundings and preparing to disintegrate it into its larger environment.

I wrote in a letter that week, "It felt so much like my life, this pile of what might be abundance in other circumstances requiring scrutiny, weeding, becoming slightly disgusting as the pile began to seep juices onto my floor and to smell a little. It felt like a living organism, a slime mold, an occupying army of apricots, as though it might multiply, as though it might move of its own accord, and it was impossible to pick it free of rot."

The Marquis de Sade himself left instructions that he was to be buried without ceremony in a grove on his country estate and that the grave was to be sown with acorns so it might disappear and the trees themselves might consume him. The earth in the form of bacteria, fungi, insects, and the other minute hordes within the soil undoubtedly devoured him, and maybe his corpse metamorphosed into oaks, though de Sade's books continued to devour trees as they kept memory of his furious, destructive, productive life from disappearing.

In those days, before corpses were injected with the poisonous preservatives that now contaminate whole cemeteries and the water tables beneath, bodies just disappeared, though dust to dust is not quite the right description for the most common sort of damp transmigration, and sometimes the bones remained. There's a legend that, when apples were planted over the grave of a seventeenth-century New England patriarch buried in his own garden, one of the trees sent down a root that devoured his body while assuming its form. The forked root is still on display in a

of their species—a packet that contains their genes to fertilize her eggs, but also

Rhode Island museum, but metamorphosis is generally more creative than that, not echoing but erasing forms and inventing other ones from the material, a kaleidoscope of atoms and molecules tumbling into new formations over and over.

Cooking is likewise a mode of transformation and a pleasure to which I often repair, and it sometimes seems so pleasurable because it is the opposite of writing; it engages all the senses; it's immediate and unreproduceable and then it's complete and eaten and over. The tasks are simple, messy, fragrant, and brief, and success and failure are easy to determine. Perhaps it's that cooking operates in the realm of biology, of things arising and falling away, sustaining bodies, while writing tries to shore up something against time and in the course of doing so appears only slowly and takes you away from the here and now.

A pie might be eaten warm from the oven by the cook and her companions but a book is read many months or years after it's written, out of sight of the writer, who never knows quite what she's done. *Ars longa, vita brevis*—art is long, life is short—used to be a popular saying, and cooking is usually on the side of life, but making preserves is an art of stalling time, of making the fruit that is so evanescent last indefinitely. To cook something is to prepare for its disappearance by devouring, the festive funeral at which it will be buried in the eater and thenceforth metamorphose into the next life and the next round of excrement and thence back to earth.

But to preserve something is to delay that act indefinitely. Maybe preserves are where a historian's urges meet a cook's capacities. I wish that I could put up yesterday's evening sky for all posterity, could preserve a night of love, the sound of a mountain

nutrients to help feed the female and create their offspring. No other kind of

stream, a realization as it sets my mind afire, a dance, a day of harmony, ten thousand glorious days of clouds that will instead vanish and never be seen again, line them up in jars where they might be admired in the interim and tasted again as needed. My historian's nature regards with dismay that all these things arise and perish, though there will always be more clouds and more days, if not for me or for you. Photographs preserve a little of this, and I've kept tens of thousands of e-mails and letters, but there is no going back.

In our machines we seek to speed everything up, but in our preserving technologies to slow down the decline of our flesh, the fading of our goods, the crumbling of our buildings, to keep out of the mouth of time all those things that she will chew up and then devour anyway. What does it matter to her hand? Time itself is our tragedy and most of us are fighting some kind of war against it. Napoléon had the Marquis de Sade arrested and imprisoned in 1801, and his family had him transferred to an insane asylum in 1803, where he remained for the eleven years until his death and burial in that grove. Napoléon's administration also offered a reward of 12,000 francs for anyone who could come up with a better way of preserving food on a grand scale.

Human beings had used drying, fermenting, salting, pickling, and, in cool climates, storing in cold cellars and, in the coldest, freezing food for later, but none of these could adequately provision a vast army. So as he prosecuted his wars against all Europe, Napoléon also sought to fight a war against decay. The confectioner and cook Nicolas Appert won the prize in 1810 after many years of experiments with sealing and boiling glass jars, pretty much the method that is still used, the one that my friend and I

animal gives a gift quite like that. People like to think about butterflies and moths

were using in my kitchen on an August evening in the twenty-first century.

I always liked canning, something I learned from the inserts that came with the cases of Ball and Kerr jars and from the worn copy of the *Joy of Cooking* my mother passed along when she got a newer one, the edition old enough to have a diagram on how to skin a squirrel and instructions on cooking possums and muskrats. I used to go to a creek near her house outside the city, spend a good part of a summer day down in the shady depths, and bring gallons of berries back to my home. Landscape is something we usually admire from a distance, but my annual day in the creek was about looking at everything up close, mostly less than the length of my arm.

I learned to recognize the ripe berries by their gleam, to recognize and skip the dull, soft berries past their prime, spot the sprays of berries that hung in the shadows of the leaves, to reach through the thorny branches with a minimum of scratching, though my hands were always purple and welted by the end, to pull the berries off so that they would not squish in my fingers. Then, after a day of looking at spiderwebs, at the small jewel-like beetles that roamed the blackberries, at minnows in the stream, and at water striders on its surface, a day of wading knee-deep in cool water and picking mint and watercress and red-orange lilies along with berries, I went home with my bounty. I poured the bowls of berries into a pot, added sugar, let the smell and steam fill the room, and made a runny, seedy form of preserves that looked black in the jars but tasted like summer in wintertime.

Those days were violet and midnight blue; this was an evening

as though they were flying flowers, but they are fierce insects, struggling through

in orange, except that that word that is the name of another fruit doesn't describe the soft color of apricots, richer than peaches, blushing red, a flush like an evening sky or a golden-skinned baby's cheek. We sorted through the huge pile on the impermeable tarp that had replaced the bedsheet, creating a big heap that would go straight into the compost and filling many of my biggest bowls with halved apricots, then trays and pots, because there was still an embarrassment of riches left over.

I cut an apricot in half, pared away any bad spots, took out the pit. Then I took up another apricot, split it along the seam—the little cleft and ridge that gives each fruit a pair of hemispheres, so that when they're ripe you can sometimes halve them neatly without tools—and then another one. In that moment when everything was falling apart and nothing was certain, a pile of fruit even that vast was pleasantly manageable by comparison. And the smell when the little hemispheres of fruit were simmering in their vanilla bath was exquisite.

In canning you first heat the contents to a temperature that will kill nearly anything that might grow on the fruit. The sugar and acids of the fruit help create an environment without microbes, and you finish off the process by putting it all in jars that have themselves been sterilized in boiling water, and put a sterilized lid on top. As the contents cool they create a vacuum that seals the jar tightly. By sterile, we mean nothing grows. Each container is a capsule in which time stands still. We put up fourteen pints in vanilla syrup that night, and then I went on and made jams and chutneys and put the many pounds left in the freezer of a nearby friend, where they would stay until her marriage broke up

each phase of life, spending time as caterpillars, bursting skins, dissolving selves in

suddenly and she moved in with me. We somehow never recovered them and they were undoubtedly thrown out. I don't remember why I didn't dry any apricots.

Even so, I tried to make the most of my birthright, my inheritance, my windfall, my fairy-tale ordeal. I had a long row of pint jars of apricots in syrup and of jam and chutney. I saved a lot of the pits and made the Italian liqueur out of apricot pits, grain alcohol, and sugar, left to sit together in the dark for three months. During that time the delicate almondlike essence at the center of the pits seeps out to flavor the liquid and somehow turns it a ruddy amber color that could be called apricot. I had learned the recipe from my friends with the big old apricot tree in their courtyard in New Mexico, the tree they dined and napped under in summertime, that I had slept under myself on a few warm nights, that in stormy springs lost all its blossoms and bore no fruit and in other years gave them more than they knew what to do with and smeared the courtyard with fallen fruit.

There's a painting of a basket of rosy apricots in the museum a few miles northwest of my home. The fruits look so firm they seem to almost float in the basket, weightless but not immortal. Several have the small flecks that might augur impending decay, and a fly is on the foremost one, exquisitely painted and undoubtedly ominous for the fate of the fruit. A couple of dark boughs of plums and leaves lie across this abundance; a peach lies to the left of the basket and a lemon to the right, while three quarter sections of a cut lemon are scattered across the foreground. Some of the carefully painted apricots still have woody stems; some have only the dents like navels where the stems broke off.

On a few of the leaves are dewdrops, gleaming like jewels,

chrysalises and cocoons, mating in various intense and lengthy ways, devouring

signs both of the ephemerality of the contents of the composition and the talent of the painter, probably Jacob van Hulsdonck, painting sometime in the first half of the seventeenth century. The label doesn't attribute the painting definitively, but other paintings by Hulsdonck even show the same wicker basket with upright stakes like bars on a window, through which more fruit can be seen. Around the corner from that painting is a more typical Golden Age Dutch still life painted by Abraham van Beyeren in a brushier manner and showing a much more lavish cascade of fruit, glassware, silver platters, bread, a cut ham, and a lobster whose right claw seems about to seize a pocket watch, though the crustacean's coral color makes it clear it's already been cooked.

The Netherlands was exploding in this era, suddenly affluent on an unprecedentedly broad social scale and amid an extraordinary flowering of the arts, particularly the art of painting. The country was expanding outward in the trade that sent Dutch ships to China and around the world; it was expanding upward with its wealth; and it was expanding inward through science. The painter Johannes Vermeer was baptized in the same Delft church the same week as Antonie van Leeuwenhoek, the man who pioneered the making and use of microscopes. His tubes with lenses, like telescopes in reverse, began to open up the miniature world of bacteria, mold, one-cell creatures, and the cells of the human body, an unsuspected universe where so much happens that affected the visible human-scale world. Recognizing the cause of so much illness and death lay centuries away, but when it was found it would be found with microscopes.

The still life with lobster by Abraham van Beyeren is supposed to be a vanitas painting because of the pocket watch, but that only

plant poisons to make themselves inedible, extending their extraordinarily long

raises the vexed question of what a vanitas painting is. Such artworks are supposed to be about the futility of human cravings, aspirations, and attachments in the face of the transience of all things. In painting, vanitas often became a parade of particular emblems, including clocks and watches, hourglasses, musical instruments, candles burning down, skulls, bubbles and children blowing bubbles, and fruit and flowers that signified impending decay or were beginning to decline already. Most were still lifes; some were domestic scenes with the appurtenances of still life.

A seventeenth-century Protestant preacher who was the bishop of Derry in northern Ireland, Ezekiel Hopkins, put it this way in a sermon titled "The Vanity of the World," which opens with the famous passage from Ecclesiastes, "Vanity of vanities; all is vanity." He comments, "For these things, though they make a fair and gaudy shew, yet it is all shew and appearance. As bubbles, blown into the air, will represent great variety of orient and glittering colors . . . so truly this world, this earth on which we live, is nothing else but a great bubble blown up by the breath of God in the midst of the air where it now hangs." The Dutch philosopher Erasmus had revived the Latin expression *homo bulla,* man is a bubble, some decades earlier, and bubbles often floated through vanitas paintings.

David Bailly, a contemporary of the apricot painter Jacob van Hulsdonck, painted a subdued still-life self-portrait, in which he in black looks back at the viewer from a seat at a table crowded with flowers, art, and a skull. A tall glass of white wine or ale stands in front of a black-and-white drawing or print of a woman, and it's a quiet demonstration of skill to show her through this

tongues at manure and puddles. Moths drink the tears of sleeping birds, and other

warping glass. Across this intimate space of solid objects float three soap bubbles. A fourth has landed next to the pearls.

Their presence makes the time in the picture not the years the painter might have looked that way or the hours or days such an arrangement of roses and inanimate objects might have lasted, but brief moments, instants even. They are the second hand of the clock in the painting, ticking time away, and hanging on to it, for a soap bubble lasts a minute and here are these four that were painted when Europeans were small, vulnerable communities of invaders in North America, when other Dutchmen looking through the first microscopes were discovering the world of animalcules, of tiny swimmers in droplet seas.

The bubble paintings were, like most vanitas paintings, supposed to be stern warnings but were also strong pleasures. In words one might describe the ephemerality of bubbles, but in paintings the moment of the bubble and its beauty persist; that basket of apricots is nearly four hundred years old and the bloom is still on the fruit; the fly has not yet done his damage; the dewdrops have not dried up. Some art historians argue the earlier emphasis on vanitas themes overinterpreted or misinterpreted the painters' intentions. Others point out that all still lifes deal in transience, whether they show fruit and flowers or skulls and bubbles. The painters seem to have found a point of equilibrium in which both were possible, the pleasure and the warning. And they seem to have moved closer to the original meaning of vanitas without knowing it.

The word *vanitas* is only a step from the English word *vanity,* which has a host of pejorative meanings. It's a word that conveys

moths feed at the eyes of deer, elephants, water buffalo. There are crocodile tears

futility, fruitlessness, and foolish pride. Sometimes the famous passage in Ecclesiastes has an even harsher interpretation: the New International version of the Bible translates it, presumably from the Latin, as meaninglessness, and turns the famous passage in Ecclesiastes into a scolding, "Utterly meaningless! Everything is meaningless," a far cry from the majestic cadences of the King James Bible's "Vanity of vanities; all is vanity."

There's a sort of decay or mutation of language at work. *Vanitas* is Latin. It means emptiness and is related to the word *vacant*. The Latin Vulgate Bible, the standard version for most of Europe for a thousand years, derives from the Greek Septuagint, where the word that occurs thirty-eight times in Ecclesiastes is *mataiotes,* which means emptiness, meaninglessness, but also transience. Does transience render all things meaningless? The Hebrew word in the original of Ecclesiastes, unavailable until modern times, when scraps of surviving manuscript were found in dry caves, is *hevel*. It means breath or vapor, and the sense of transience is vivid but the condemnation of the transient is nowhere to be found.

Ezekiel Hopkins's "a great bubble blown up by the breath of God" and all those paintings of children blowing bubbles return to the original meaning, for each breath is fleeting but breathing is life itself. There's a story about a Zen student who complains that paying attention to his breath and counting his breaths, the fundamental exercise of Zen meditation, is boring. His teacher plunges his head into a stream and holds it down a long moment, then pulls him up and says, "Still boring?" Less boring when its transience is more evident.

Years ago I visited a friend who lived on a houseboat and while

and moths that feed upon them. In the forests of Southeast Asia several species that

admiring the lemon trees and prickly pears flourishing ferociously in half-barrel planters on his deck was told that the deck was forever rotting away from the dampness and had to be replaced at least once a decade. As we walked down the long plank boardwalk back to shore, we talked about whether humidity and aridity themselves could have been forces that shaped religious belief. There are in many damp places a belief in reincarnation, the eternal renewing of life and the world, which of course also means eternal dying. In the warm, damp regions everything disintegrates, regenerates, must be rebuilt, manuscripts must be copied over as the pages decay, and the air is full of spores and bacterias and insects eager to consume and transmute.

In the dry world you can at least fantasize about unchanging permanence and eternity, and bodies can be mummified, preserved by drying—like fruit, fish, books in libraries, the Dead Sea scrolls, and paintings in climate-controlled museums. In the cold world things may also last for ages, like those frozen bodies of mammoths and mountaineers. The photographer Irving Penn made a witty modern still life out of blocks of frozen food—raspberries, blueberries, asparagus, carrots, beans, pale under a haze of frost—standing on end, an architecture that must have already been thawing and on its way to collapse under the studio lights.

I preserved the apricots that August, and my friend who had helped me with the first round of canning badgered me to have my first mammogram a few months later, only about six weeks after the terrible turbulence of September and the invitation to Iceland. In those days every woman over forty was supposed to have one annually; I was years behind that schedule, though a few

feed at the eyes of human beings were documented by the patient entomologist

years later the guidelines would shift and suggest that some of us could wait until fifty, but by then it was too late for me. I went dutifully but dismissively to be irradiated by those machines whose vises clasp your breasts like a lobster clamping onto a clock. Everything in my family history and my own habits exonerated me from danger, and I expected this business of making images of me from the inside would do the same. It didn't.

I didn't see the first round of pictures from the standard exam, but they were apparently interesting enough that my nurse-practitioner, who had also urged me to get examined and saw the results, moved up my biopsy date. And so it was that I found myself one afternoon two weeks later lying facedown on a table, cautioned not to move for the next hour, with a major section of myself anesthetized, and the whirring sound of a tiny drill entering my flesh again and again through the hole in the table. From where I lay, in a position that became excruciating because I had to hold it so long, I could twist my neck and see a screen where images of that breast in black and white showed huge on a monitor.

What size is a representation? No size at all, for we get used to seeing satellite photographs of continents the same size as snapshots of babies. These images looked like a night sky, hemispheres of darkness with pale streaky strands like clouds or vapor or the Milky Way in a desert night when the stars are so numerous they blur into radiant fields. Some of the bright areas, the microcalcifications or tiny calcium deposits that looked pale in that dark sky, were the grounds for concern.

On the screen that day was an image that didn't look at all like me. It was me, and my fate, this mortal heaven they were

Hans Bänziger, who remained still while they found him and fed at his, as he

exploring with instruments, guided by live X-ray images, working remotely, as though they were embarked upon a moon probe or an ocean-floor exploration. Pearls, bubbles, skulls, bowls of fruit, but in my case it was interior images; a portion of my body that had always been there had been numbed into nonexistence, and a version of my body that had never existed before, that strange night sky on the screen, had supplanted it. I was not here but there, in this new vanitas picture.

The procedure on the table was a stereotactic core biopsy, and the device I was lying upon made the digital images I saw on the screen, and the images guided the cluster of people hovering around me about where to drill next for the thin core samples of flesh that would be examined later under a microscope. A pathologist would look at my cells to see if some of the cells in the lining of the milk ducts had begun to stray from their intended pattern. That is, if I had cancer.

Or rather had anomalous cells that might or might not become cancer, might have "ductal carcinomas in situ," as they're called. Some go on to become invasive cancers; some don't; and no one yet can predict which are which. Twenty years ago these cells were too subtle to be detected by X-rays; in another ten or twenty, medical technology will likely be able to determine which go on to be invasive. At that point in time, their presence could be detected but not their prospects, so they were all regarded as perilous. My portrait was being painted by digital X-ray machines from the inside out and by microscope slides from the cellular level up; it was a portrait of mortality. Of course I had always been mortal, but not quite so emphatically so.

I was being pared like an apricot with a bad spot, or rather a

reported in "Remarkable New Cases of Moths Drinking Human Tears in

bad spot was being sought in the outer space under my skin. And this was only the beginning. The voyage I was to go on was a tour of a country where many go much farther and some don't return. I had thought Iceland was my next major journey, but this other country was on the route beforehand. In this country, you are yourself the terrain, and you are traveling toward or away from your mortality. You do not know yourself, but must rely on expert guides and interpreters. More than that, you are not yourself.

You must be patient, must become a patient, must take up residence in waiting rooms, must learn to wait for experts and results, must grow accustomed to being laid out upon tables and invaded, described in unfamiliar language, and treated with methods that may seem like illnesses and injuries though they are intended to cure. Your life is a ship others steer; it contains mysteries you do not understand; those mysteries include that eventuality when you are no longer yourself at all, whether these sailors save you from it for the time being or just hold you at the top of the waterfall for a while.

The real story of your life is always all the way from birth to death, and the medical experts appear like oracles to interpret and guide even as they turn you from your familiar self, a dealer in stories, into mute meat, breathing or approaching last breaths. They often look away from you to make and interpret the maps of the world beneath your skin by which they navigate. Portraits and descriptions of you amass in folders you might be allowed to see, or not. You may need interpreters even to understand the scrawled notes and test results. You are your biological self, a vast and enigmatic landscape of interiors, flows, chemistry, cells,

Thailand" in the Natural History Bulletin of the Siam Society *twenty years*

systems, and samples. You exist as a few cells under a microscope and on a chart of statistics for your categories.

All of the images they make of you are vanitas images, reminders of your frailty and the fleetingness of all things, particularly your own flesh, a bubble sustained by breath. The singer of Federico García Lorca's "Somnambule Ballad," blood like roses blooming on his shirt, asks for refuge, but his friend, who suffers from a more enigmatic condition, replies: *"Pero yo ya no soy yo, ni mi casa es ya mi casa."* But I am no longer I, nor is my house still my house. House, country, landscape, kingdom of the body, now strange and foreign.

---

back. He photographed one drinking from his own right eye with its furry wings

6 · Wound

A couple of years earlier, I was the one who offered to take home the very old woman, a friend of my friend, but the boyfriend who deserted during my crises, or fell apart during his, was the one who actually drove her across town. She was worn out from the political conference, but still lively enough to tell us about her adventures in Cuba forty years earlier, where she had met Che Guevara. That a figure so legendary had crossed paths with the tired woman with the creased cheeks and dyed black hair in the front passenger seat was a little astonishing, as it always is when what seems like the remote and mythic past turns out to be within reach of someone present. They started talking about the Che movie.

That feature film, *The Motorcycle Diaries,* after Ernesto "Che" Guevara's journal of the same name, makes the medical student and his young doctor friend Alberto Granado seem like dharma bums, drifting around the Latin American continent for general adventure, but their purpose was a little more pointed. In 1950 Granado was already working in a leprosy hospital in Córdoba, Argentina, and his friend had joined him there for several days, then set out on a solo adventure on motorcycle. Though he returned to medical school, his appetite for wandering was whetted, and Guevara and Granado set out on their grand motorcycle expedition two years later.

outspread, looking like a tremendous tear or a misplaced brooch or a flower petal,

They traveled across the Andes, up the west coast and into the Amazon from leprosarium to leprosarium, and even in between presented themselves to hospitals and townspeople as experts in the disease. Afterward Granado returned to the field, in a leprosy hospital in Venezuela, and invited Guevara to join him. Guevara even published a couple of scholarly papers on the disease and wrote his parents toward the end of that odyssey, "I've become really interested in leprology, but I don't know how long it will last. . . ."

That long road trip on the motorcycle that kept breaking down and was eventually abandoned is how and when Guevara woke up to a particular kind of pain himself and then to his sense of purpose on earth. He encountered the destitute, the dispossessed, the dying, and the outcast—an unemployed miner and his wife shivering without blankets in the Chilean desert, an old woman dying of asthma and poverty, indigenous girls and women groped by soldiers, the pariahs of the leper colonies in the Amazon jungle. He was not quite twenty-five, a handsome, spoiled firstborn son of an upper-class Argentinean family who approached almost everything with an air of scorn and feigned indifference, who took pleasure in offending hosts and violating conventions.

One of his biographers, Jon Lee Anderson, speculates that he had chosen to become a doctor because he watched his grandmother die in agony, but he delayed his exams and took his studies casually. He had known pain long before, and illness, and the nearness of death, lived all his life in and out of that country of the sick. He had since early childhood been prone to brutal asthma attacks. At any moment his bronchial passages might seize up, breathing might become almost impossible, and his whole body racked with pain. Death was always a possibility.

an ornament invading his face. When another species came and drank, "I then

This may have contributed to his savage debonairness, his air of a hero who dared much and feared little. Even on the trip with Granado he often had dangerous attacks that his friend would rescue him from with a big shot of adrenaline. And even with this drastic treatment he would often be unable to function for several hours or a day or more. His health was a bomb that often went off. Maybe asthma was the deus ex machina at the Cuban Revolution.

Doctors help people; they diagnose them; sometimes they alleviate their pain; sometimes they cure them. But they do it one by one, and the causes they address seldom include social or economic conditions. The young Guevara diagnosed the continent and the world as suffering from a disease produced by injustice and prescribed revolution for it, a cure as violent as any surgery. But the diagnosis took a long time and planning his future did too. Step by step he veered from thinking he would continue with medicine.

He did receive his medical degree not long after the motorcycle odyssey but immediately embarked upon further travels across the continent. He then imagined what a revolutionary doctor would be and dreamed of a medicine that would create "a robust body through the work of the whole collectivity, especially the social collectivity." He and Granado had met a communist doctor who was a leprosy specialist, Hugo Pesce, in Lima, Peru, and Pesce became an important influence on Guevara, both by the example of his commitments and his compassion, and by dispatching the young medics to the leprosy in the rain forest of the uppermost Amazon River.

On that adventure, his environment changed; it let in things that he had not encountered or had encountered but not assessed

caught the moth by cautiously lowering the wide net over my head and the

or felt before. "I began to come into close contact with poverty, with hunger, with disease, with the inability to cure a child because of a lack of resources, with the numbness that hunger and continued punishment cause. . . . And I began to see that there was something that, at that time, seemed to me almost as important as being a famous researcher or making some substantial contribution to medical science, and this was helping those people."

Out of empathy for the sufferers he met on his odyssey, the young man evolved into one of the great revolutionary icons of the twentieth century. He became the public figure the old woman we drove home met when she was young herself. But it was my then-boyfriend on that drive across town who astonished me more by telling us in the course of the conversation about *The Motorcycle Diaries* that it was not the disease of leprosy itself that caused so much damage to hands and feet. The disease strangles nerves, kills off feeling, and what you cannot feel you cannot take care of: not the disease but the patient does the damage. You begin nicking, burning, bruising, abrading, and otherwise wearing out your fingers, toes, feet, hands, and then losing them.

Pain serves a purpose. Without it you are in danger. What you cannot feel you cannot take care of. It seemed shockingly accurate at the time, a new and brutal version of an old truth, so I read up on leprosy and on pain. A young woman named Yolanda in one of the first leprosy colonies Guevara visited liked to protest that she should not be there because there was nothing wrong with her. Since she was beautiful and without obvious signs of illness, people tended to take up her cause. Guevara began to argue with Granado, her physician, until the latter showed that a hypodermic stuck into one of the numbed patches on her back elicited no

moth." Moths drink the tears. The word for teardrinkers is lachryphagous, *and*

reaction. The younger man was furious and accused his friend of using her to show off and then gradually accepted that she was ill despite her attractions. She didn't feel the needle, but he did.

Leprosy is a bacterial infection to which most of us are immune and the small percentage who aren't have a hard time catching—it is among the most incommunicable of communicable diseases, and when you catch it, many years may pass before symptoms appear, making the method of contagion a little mysterious even now. Those who contract it sometimes have only minor symptoms on their skin; or they have disfiguring skin rashes, eruptions and growths, and those areas grow numb; or they sustain more extensive nerve damage. The leprosy bacillus is particularly at home in the cooler parts of the body, the skin, the hands, the forearms, the feet and lower legs, and the nose and eyes. In almost any of these places, infected nerves can swell up and then strangle in their sheath and die.

The nerveless part of the body remains alive, but pain and sensation define the self; what you cannot feel is not you; what you cannot feel you do not readily take care of; your extremities become lost to you. Pain protects; you get something in your eyes, and you do something about it, but delicately, gingerly, or it hurts. You flinch, you blink, tears flow. With leprosy, you might stop blinking, so your eyes go dry, or you rub them too hard and scar the cornea, or fail to notice some injury at all. Thus blindness is a common consequence of the disease.

For centuries the infection ravaged people around the world, from India to Iceland. It was a Norwegian doctor with a microscope who identified it in 1873 as being caused by a bacteria—it was in fact the first such disease identified this way. Hansen's

for the eaters of human flesh it is anthropophagous, *and the rest of us feed on*

disease, after this pioneer doctor, is the more polite term for the disorder, but almost no one knows what Hansen's disease is. People don't really know what leprosy is either, when it comes to the details.

Before Hansen, the disease was thought to be hereditary, or easily transmitted, or transmitted sexually, or acquired as a punishment for sins and sexual corruption, or to be a spiritual disorder that marked the sufferers out as chosen in some harsh way for redemption through suffering. During the Second World War, the disease became curable with an extended course of sulfone drugs, and millions have since been cured by that and then more-sophisticated and less-toxic drug regimes. Not everyone who contracts the disease receives the treatment, and there are still leper colonies and outcasts around the world.

Those with leprosy in most times and places were cast out, isolated, quarantined in the United States well into the 1960s and beyond, or even driven out to die while people with much more contagious diseases, from syphilis to tuberculosis, were not subjected to any such treatment. Native Hawaiians, who were in the nineteenth century hunted down and forced into the remote leper colony beneath the great cliff at Molokai if they had the disease, called it "the separating sickness."

The stigma was so great that families lied that the afflicted member had died. Leprosy was grounds for divorce. In the United States in the twentieth century, people were encouraged to change their names when they went into quarantine, as though their old, free self had died. To receive the diagnosis of leprosy was to be cast out of society, and most never came back. Leprosy was really two diseases, a bacterial infection and a social stigma, and the latter,

sorrow all the time. It is the essence of many of the most beautiful ballads and pop

the separation sickness, was often the most painful and debilitating. They suffered like Frankenstein's creature the terrible exile of the abhorred.

It was another doctor with a strong sense of purpose, Paul Brand, who confirmed and taught that the disease itself didn't cause much of the damage by which it's known. He was a missionary doctor in India who began working with leprosy patients as a skilled surgeon, helping to uncurl contracted fingers and otherwise tending to the wounds and disfigurements of the disease. When the disease became curable, Brand wondered why even the cured patients continued to lose joints or whole digits of hands and feet and to acquire more injuries and infections.

His investigations revealed that it was due to numbness: you might hold the match or the cigarette until it burned your fingers, touch the too-hot iron, hold the tool with the sharp edge that gouged your hand, wear the badly fitting shoes until they rubbed holes into your feet, and then ignore the resulting damage and infection. Your self is what you feel, and for those with leprosy that sense of self retreated up the hand or arm or leg as the extremities went numb.

Some of the Indian youths Brand treated described their hands as no longer part of themselves, and his job was to teach them to take care of these insensible, alienated limbs with the kindness with which they might tend someone else. "But I am no more I, nor is my house still my house." In this part of the kingdom of the sick, the borders are blurry. Brand wrote, "Sometimes I felt like a schoolmaster, with the odd sense that I was introducing the boys to their own limbs, begging their minds to welcome the insensitive parts of their bodies. It was easy to think of the boys as being

songs, and why sorrow and heartbreak are so delicious might have to do with the

careless or irresponsible until I began to understand their point of view.

"Pain, along with its cousin touch, is distributed universally on the body, providing a sort of boundary of *self*. Even after surgery, they tended to view their repaired hands and feet as tools or artificial appendages. They lacked the basic instinct of self-protection that pain normally provides. One of the boys said to me, 'My hands and feet don't feel part of me. They are like tools I can use. But they aren't really me. I can see them, but in my mind they are dead.' I heard similar comments often, underscoring the crucial role pain plays in unifying the human body."

Physical pain is often lonely, felt only by one person who must trust that others will believe and empathize, and convincing doctors of pain is one of the tasks of the sufferer without overt symptoms or causes. Leprosy can cause excruciating pain, and it can also cause the painlessness that means even the sufferer doesn't feel injury. Empathy is the capacity to feel what you do not literally feel, and Brand taught his young patients a kind of empathy for the extremities that no longer seemed part of themselves. "I feel for you," people say. If pain defines the boundaries of the body, you participate in the social body with those you empathize with, whose pain pains you—and whose joy is also contagious.

Some empathy must be learned and then imagined, by perceiving the suffering of others and translating it into one's own experience of suffering and thereby suffering a little with them. Empathy can be a story you tell yourself about what it must be like to be that other person; but its lack can also arise from narrative, about why the sufferer deserved it, or why that person or those people have nothing to do with you. Whole societies can be taught

emotions it stirs in us, the empathy for others' suffering, and the small comfort of

to deaden feeling, to disassociate from their marginal and minority members, just as people can and do erase the humanity of those close to them.

Empathy makes you imagine the sensation of the torture, of the hunger, of the loss. You make that person into yourself, you inscribe their suffering on your own body or heart or mind, and then you respond to their suffering as though it were your own. Identification, we say, to mean that I extend solidarity to you, and who and what you identify with builds your own identity. Physical pain defines the physical boundaries of the self but these identifications define a larger self, a map of affections and alliances, and the limits of this psychic self are nothing more or less than the limits of love. Which is to say love enlarges; it annexes affectionately; at its utmost it dissolves all boundaries.

When I became fascinated by the implications of leprosy, I first thought of those who felt nothing for themselves. Those who suffer are considered to be worse off than those who don't, but those who suffer can care for themselves, protect themselves, seek change, prevent further injury, and recover. The poet Rainer Maria Rilke called the sufferings that are drowned out "spurned, lost life, of which one may die."

If the boundaries of the self are defined by what we feel, then those who cannot feel even for themselves shrink within their own boundaries, while those who feel for others are enlarged, and those who feel compassion for all beings must be boundless. They are not separate, not alone, not lonely, not vulnerable in the same way as those of us stranded in the islands of ourselves, but they are vulnerable in other ways. Still, that sense of the dangers of feeling for others is so compelling that many withdraw, and develop

not being alone with our own. With a sad song we feel a delicate grief, as though

elaborate stories to justify withdrawal, and then forget that they have shrunk. Most of us do, one way or another.

Those with leprosy lose their own boundaries another way as they lose sensation, and sometimes the body itself falls away as it becomes unfelt and then unprotected and untended. But this is only physical pain, the pain that defines the boundaries of the corporeal self. Granado wrote, "The scourge of leprosy forces its victims out of society and at the same time makes them particularly sensitive and grateful."

In one section of his poem "Howl," Allen Ginsberg cries out over and over, "I'm with you in Rockland" to his friend Carl Solomon trapped in the psychiatric hospital, meaning that he's with him in solidarity, that they are not separate, and the assertion itself sounds across the distance. And then the poet rescues his friend in a final line of that section of the poem, "in my dreams you walk dripping from a sea-journey on the highway across America in tears to the door of my cottage in the Western night."

We're close, we say, to mean that we're emotionally connected, that we are not separate; or, we've become distant, to describe the opposite. After years in New York City, Georgia O'Keeffe moved to rural New Mexico, from which she would sign her letters to the people she loved, "from the faraway nearby." It was a way to measure physical and psychic geography together. Emotion has its geography, affection is what is nearby, within the boundaries of the self. You can be a thousand miles from the person next to you in bed or deeply invested in the survival of a stranger on the other side of the world.

Paul Brand wrote, "I believe that this quality of shared pain is what it means to be a human being." To injure, to kill, to cause

we mourn for three minutes a loss we can't remember but taste again, sorrow like

suffering in others, requires first that withdrawal of empathy that would have made such action painful or impossible, and to intentionally cause pain in others requires you to kill yourself off a little in the process. Some undertake that process willingly, if unwittingly, while soldiers are often forced to undergo some version of it as training and as wartime. Surviving the horrific is likewise often done by shutting down sensation, by becoming numb to one's own pain.

When the psychiatrist Robert Jay Lifton went to investigate the psychology of survivors of the atomic bombing of Hiroshima and Nagasaki, he coined the term "psychic numbing" to describe the survival strategy of disassociation and apathy—"a diminished capacity or inclination to feel." In such extreme circumstances it was necessary or at least understandable, but even there Lifton called it "dehumanization" and cautioned that it "comes to resemble what has been called 'miscarried repair.'" He compared it to autoimmune disorders that begin by eradicating hostile outside organisms and then turn on the body itself.

You erected a wall between yourself and annihilation or horror and sometimes it then walled you off from life. The wall itself sometimes grew like a disease if left untreated. Those with leprosy lose only physical sensation; it is the rest of us who tend to lose moral, emotional sensation around their suffering. Which is to say that leprosy was for millennia a psychological disorder of whole societies, though it was a bacterial infection of only a minority.

If numbness contracts the boundaries of the self, empathy expands it. You can describe what happened to Guevara in the trip across the leprosariums of South America as an awakening, but you can also think of it as an enlarging; he took the people he met

salt tears, and then close it up like a letter in the final notes. Sadness the blue like

in, into himself, and his boundaries moved outward. When he and Granado met the shivering couple in the Chilean desert, they gave away one of their two blankets. They sometimes gave nothing more than attention and affection, and they were given much in return. As they left the leprosy hospital in Lima, the patients bade them a fond farewell: "They had all chipped in 100½ soles, which they gave to us with an effusive letter. Afterwards some of them came to say goodbye to us personally and in more than one case tears were shed. . . . If there's anything that will make us seriously dedicate ourselves to leprosy, it will be the affection shown to us by all the sick we've met along the way."

The young men were hardly saints. They lied a little and pumped up their roles as leprologists to get food and lodgings, and hustled a lot to get into bed with the women they met along the way, usually to no avail. They drank when the opportunity arose, ran away from unpaid bills, shot a beloved dog by accident, and bumbled along making messes that others would clean up, as young men often do. But they were kind to the sufferers they met. In the leprosarium they lingered in the longest, they broke with precedent by touching the patients without barriers such as gloves and later by playing soccer with them.

Granado writes, "Then we went to see another patient, a former teacher at a nearby school. She was very moved when we greeted her with a handshake and sat on the same chairs she sat on, and her tears—a blend of sorrow and happiness—moved us too." This was the leprosy colony in the jungle of the headwaters of the Amazon, where the doctors and staff lived on one side of the river and the patients on another. In what seems to have been an epochal act in his life, Guevara jumped in the broad river and

dusk, the reminder that all things are ephemeral, and that because there is time

swam across it, toward them. The river was a physical space that had become a psychic space, and in crossing the one he crossed the other and arrived at some firmer sense of self and solidarity.

Several years later, during the invasion of Cuba by Castro's small, ragged band of guerrillas, Guevara had another pivotal moment in the midst of heavy gunfire. He had to choose whether to take his first-aid kit or a box of bullets as he fled. He took the ammunition and in taking it crossed back over that river in some sense. He had become a revolutionary out of the most tender-hearted empathy for the suffering he encountered in particular men and women. As a revolutionary he became hardhearted, dedicated to humanity in the abstract and often callous with the individuals met en route.

Guevara became a guerrilla leader, known for being harsh with his men, and he assumed a leader's right to mete out punishments. He wrote about a moment in the campaign when by their own rules someone had to execute a Cuban who had betrayed them to the government soldiers. No one wanted to. "I ended the problem [by] giving him a shot with a .32 pistol in the right side of the brain, with exit orifice in the right temporal. He gasped a little while and was dead. . . . We slept badly, wet and I with something of asthma."

Doctors take oaths not to kill or harm, but they often cause pain and commit violence upon the body with drugs and with scalpels. They learn to subdue, to cut, to inflict pain for the sake of healing and for life, and to deliver bad news. The end justifies these means. To succeed in their profession, they have to strike a balance between empathy and separation, closeness and distance, to find the right distance at which to function best for their own and the patients'

there is change and that another name for change, if you look back toward what

well-being. Like parents, they sometimes must do what is unpleasant, and they grow accustomed to others' discomfort.

Hubris is a doctor's danger, and one way to read *Frankenstein* is as a tale about a medical student's arrogance and lack of empathy. In Guevara's time, doctors also made decisions on behalf of their patients and sometimes kept them in the dark—patients with cancer were not always told their diagnosis, for example. A revolution in medical care was part of the great antiauthoritarian revolutions of the 1960s and after, a revolution whereby patients insisted on their rights to be fully informed and to participate in decisions.

The Marxist revolutionaries of the past assumed a similar paternalistic privilege of acting on behalf of peoples who might not particularly agree with the actions or the goals. The vanguard was supposed to lead the revolution and the masses eventually to wake up and follow. It was the end that justified many means. Che wrote to his children, "The true revolutionary is guided by a great feeling of love," but what that love was for is opaque. He became one of the harshest parts of a harsh regime. All this was unimaginable to the young man who gave a blanket to a cold unemployed miner and his wife and empathized with a pretty girl stranded in a leprosarium.

I think of empathy as a kind of music Guevara had caught the sound of, the "still sad music of humanity," as Wordsworth once called it, and then he became deaf to it, a dancer falling out of step. The Cuban Revolution might have been his great moment, when he united his sense of purpose with the intensity of the experience of war. Afterward Che, as he was then known, became a minister of various things, but a restless minister at odds at times with the revolution's commander, Fidel Castro. He tried to foment

is vanishing in the distance, is loss. But sadness is also beautiful, maybe because it

revolution in the Congo in 1965, with little immediate effect, and then in a backwater of Bolivia in 1967. It was as though he wanted to go back to that moment of becoming rather than live with what the revolution became.

He went to Bolivia to overthrow the government with a handful of men and no popular support. He and his small band of guerrillas were lost, dirty, desperate, and hungry, adventurers run aground in a hard land. They appeared to the isolated peasants as supernatural beings, and those last days unfolded like a folktale. One woman told the army that she thought they were *brujos,* or witches, and she imagined that the money with which they bought food would, like fairy gold, "turn worthless in her hands." Che rode a horse, smoked a pipe of silver, was dressed in rags but wore two Rolexes, and was evidently failing physically. His men had to help him off his mount. It was as though his body could not live up to the legend he was endeavoring to become, or remain.

Anderson recounts, "He no longer even had boots; instead, his mud-caked feet were encased in crude leather sheaths, like those a medieval peasant might have worn." He was captured, bound hand and foot, and left overnight on the dirt floor of a schoolhouse, and in the morning of October 9, 1967, he was shot to death. The CIA agent who shot him suddenly found that he could hardly breathe, and all the rest of his days suffered from such trouble. He came to believe that somehow Che's asthma had passed on to him. A glamour of the supernatural hovered around those last days, but it was no substitute for the navigational power of empathy.

It was a strange arc, Ernesto Guevara's life, from the great empathic awakening to the triumphant taking up of arms on

rings so true and goes so deep, because it is about the distances in our lives, the

behalf of the poor to the series of drifts that landed him in Bolivia in an unsupported insurrection doomed to fail. Fail in all practical senses, though in a less practical one, Bolivia was where Che rode a horse into his own legend and disappeared, like the T'ang Dynasty artist Wu Daozi who strolled into a painted landscape.

Maybe it's the transmutation of a living man into a legend that the locals felt as supernatural or otherworldly. You can still see in the photographs of his bare-chested corpse laid out with its beard and matted hair and faraway look in its eyes why the local women thought he looked like Christ and snipped off bits of his hair as relics. After his death "Che" came to mean one infinitely glamorous image of a fierce resolute face with shaggy hair and a beret bearing a comandante's star. *Pero yo ya no soy yo, ni mi casa es ya mi casa.* The image was reduced to a map of dark and light areas, as though Che's face had become at that moment of the photograph a strange new country. This is the image that still travels everywhere and is particularly common on T-shirts, as though the beating heart beneath had chosen a face.

That image taken by photographer Alberto Korda on March 5, 1960, is far more widespread than is knowledge of Che Guevara's life. It means everything and anything. *Guerrillero Heroico,* the posthumous face that came to represent revolution's ferocious spirit, may be the most reproduced photograph of all time. Dr. Guevara made a marvel or a monster named Che, and the monster and his magnificent glare became immortal.

When *The Motorcycle Diaries* was being filmed, Che's companion Alberto Granado came along as an adviser. He wrote, "But nothing was as deeply felt as the meeting with several of the

things we lose, the abyss between what the lover and the beloved want and

patients afflicted with leprosy who remembered our stay at the leprosarium of San Pablo—and this peaked when the youngest of them (who back in 1952 was fifteen years old) recalled the moment in which I shook his hand without putting on gloves when we met and said affectionately: 'After you two visited our hospital, people were kinder to us.' "

Granado concluded, "What greater reward could one ask from life?"

I found leprosy useful for thinking about everything else, for thinking about how my mother had gone numb in some way, so that I became the limb that could not be felt. I wonder whether it was fear of her own pain as it might extend and recur in me. Though if I was a mirror it must have been herself she saw and lashed out against. She was often kind to others. It was a wry irony that this tale of the true nature of leprosy, that made me think so much about empathy, was told to me by a man whose affection and trustworthiness failed me when I was most hard-pressed myself, because of that mother.

Of course we all turn away in various ways, if more mildly. As I write, I'm troubled by two people I'm delaying writing back to, or three. I delete several unopened e-mails a day for causes ranging from endangered animals to political prisoners, because there is more out there than I can take on, even as a reader. To feel for someone enlarges the self and then that self shares risks and pains. Or to feel for something, since the last half century has seen a vast expansion of concern and compassion for the nonhuman world, for animals, species, places, ecosystems, and finally the earth itself.

The self is a patchwork of the felt and the unfelt, of presences

imagine and understand that may widen to become unbridgeable at any moment,

and absences, of navigable channels around the walled-off numbnesses. Perhaps it's impossible for anyone short of an enlightened being to carry the weight of all suffering, even to recognize and embrace it, but we make ourselves large or small, here or there, in our empathies. I met a Thai Buddhist saint once who for twenty years took on tiny tokens and charms people gave him so that he would carry their suffering. Eventually he wore a cloak of a couple hundred pounds of clanking, chiming griefs at all times, and then it became too heavy or he'd carried it far enough, and he put it down. At the end of his talk he threw out tiny charms of his own, and I caught and kept one, a tiny golden Buddha in a small plastic bubble. I carried its imperceptible weight for many years until my purse was stolen out of my car while I was walking on a mountain.

The uses of empathy and pain were something I began to wonder about anew, when people began to drill into my flesh, to pursue me with knives. It was not long after the US Army had been torturing people in a prison in Iraq. On this table on which I lay still and listened to the drill and then stayed longer as a stout doctor with a sweet Irish accent chatted with me and tried to staunch a little stream of blood that would not stop flowing, I thought of those elaborate tortures in the American-run prison in Iraq. It was as though I was in a version of Abu Ghraib run by angels, for I was being injured for the sake of my survival by professionals with endless altruism, and there was more to come.

the distance between the hope at the outset and the eventual outcome,

7 · Knot

"If I haven't put it clearly enough, the condition they've detected is like having something ticking inside me that could turn out to be a clock without even an alarm or could be a bomb set to go off at some much later date," I wrote to the people close to me when I got the first round of diagnoses. "At this point in history, they can identify the ticking but not whether or not it's a bomb, so they treat it as though it were one."

I was beginning to meet my bomb-defusing team, the beautiful Asian oncology surgeon; the big amiable plastic surgeon; the solid, synagogue-attending head of nursing, who had the most unwaveringly attentive gaze I ever met outside of a lover; and a succession of nurses and aides, mostly devoted. I was beginning to inhabit the spaces of that other world where people weighed and measured and sampled me and wrote reports, as though I was a newly discovered island or a crime.

Afterward I referred to it all as my medical adventure, because I was unsure how else to describe a series of events in which I was not sick or injured in any perceptible way at the inception, but would be damaged and repaired by doctors. I was not even sure if I was going to qualify as a cancer survivor, since the condition they told me I had was in some versions only a potential precursor, though it was an invitation to think about mortality and

the journeys we have to travel, including the last one out of being and on past embodiment and to spend time in some of the places to which cancer takes you.

Life was in those days grim; I marched forward in determination to move through the ordeals that had sprung up one after another and come out the other end. I was old enough to know that I would and that the grimness was passing weather, but it didn't pass rapidly. Now I can see that I was going to be remade, and the timing seemed good after the ordeals of the season before.

During that strange strained phase, I was fascinated by the surgeons. They seemed like gods, since they were going to exert such power over my life, going to see me as I would never see myself, take me in hand as raw material and promise to improve my odds by doing so. I propitiated the knife-wielding deities with presents of books. The gifts to them and the head of nursing were also meant to acknowledge that although people get paid to do their jobs, you cannot pay someone to do their job passionately and wholeheartedly. Those qualities are not for sale; they are themselves gifts that can only be given freely, and are in many, many fields.

Gods and artisans, since all the cool abstract science of modern medicine was going to devolve into their handiwork on my flesh, on cutting and sewing as though I was a garment to be remade. To cut and sew flesh was a peculiar craft, and to be their fabric required faith and trust. I studied them and got a faint sense of what it might mean to be one of these people involved in the fierce intimacy of other peoples' living and dying. My work matters, I believe, but it seemed so much more remote than theirs. In their work I was the text to be interpreted and the raw material to be refabricated, and the stakes were my long-term odds of survival.

becoming into the unimaginable: the moth flown into the pure dark. Or the

I wrote to a friend that I was going to be cured of more than I had been diagnosed with. I was going to have to give up being unstoppable. I asked for help. I was not much in the habit of doing so. There were extremely unhelpful parents in my particular past, but asking is difficult for a lot of people. It's partly because we imagine that gifts put us in the giver's debt, and debt is supposed to be a bad thing. You see it in the way people sometimes try to reciprocate immediately out of a sense that indebtedness is a burden. But there are gifts people yearn to give and debts that tie us together.

Sometimes to accept is also a gift. The anthropologist David Graeber points out that the explanation that we invented money because barter was too clumsy is false. It wasn't that I was trying to trade sixty sweaters for the violin you'd made when you didn't really need all that wooliness. Before money, Graeber wrote, people didn't barter but gave and received as needs and goods ebbed and flowed. They thereby incurred the indebtedness that bound them together, and reciprocated slowly, incompletely, in the ongoing transaction that is a community. Money was invented as a way to sever the ties by completing the transactions that never needed to be completed in the older system, but existed like a circulatory system in a body. Money makes us separate bodies, and maybe it teaches us that we should be separate.

I once read an account about a wealthy Turkana man in Kenya's Rift Valley who offered to slaughter a goat in his guest's honor and then used one of his impoverished neighbor's few poor animals instead of a goat from his own large herd. The guest was perplexed, but the man who had offered his neighbor's goat eventually explained that he was thereby weaving him into the web of

flame. Australia's endangered golden sun moth lives a long time underground,

obligation and future gifts, strengthening his ties and his position, earning for him goodwill that was better than goats. The goods would continue to flow in both directions, but the immaterial goods mattered more and in losing his goat the poor man became a little richer. The host became someone he could go to for help and eventually did, receiving far more than a single goat.

Goodwill is something you put away like preserves, for a rainy day, for winter, for lean times, and it was moving to find that I had more than I had ever imagined. People gathered from all directions, and I was taken care of beautifully. My friend Antonia stepped in to manage the traffic. Afterward, during my convalescence, I occasionally wished that life was always like this, that I was always being showered with flowers and assistance and solicitousness, but you only get it when you need it. If you're lucky, you get it when you need it. To know that it was there when I needed it changed everything a little in the long run.

Even after losing the perfidious boyfriend and successfully parking the parent, it would have been easy to go back to the old ways, but this was a more definitive rupture in how I functioned. I canceled and rescheduled things, delayed the delivery of the book I was writing, said that I couldn't and asked if people could. Those people showed up in a thousand ways. The handsomest and most beautiful among them decided to tell me about damage their own clothes concealed, about lumps and cysts and scars and embarrassing ailments and anomalies you would never suspect.

My friend Pam, a family physician, serendipitously moved to my city to take a new job the week I got the first biopsy results back and took me out to dinner to explain them and alleviate some of my alarm. She showed up afterward in immensely kind

feeding on the roots of wallaby grass, and then metamorphoses into a diurnal

and skillful ways. Other female friends decided I should not go to any further appointments alone, so I was thenceforth always accompanied. I thought this crisis would be regarded as women's business, but men showed up for me too. Among them was a tough older writer who had been my friend for a dozen years; he appointed himself my Irish mother when he heard the news. He was the one who detected my lowest point and jumped in to haul me out of it.

I gave away a lot of the apricots that winter, bottles of preserves and chutney and the elixir or liqueur that was finally ready, exquisite high-proof stuff that had turned golden during its months in the dark and acquired a delicate almond flavor. A bottle of it went to my friend Tom, who quickly welded a shower curtain holder for my eccentric tub because I was going to be forbidden baths for a while, and a bottle to Sam, who told me to get over being squeamish and give him the necessary details to make him useful, a bottle to Marina, to Amy, to my younger brother, and jars of apricots in vanilla syrup to various people, including Nellie and Ann.

These last two friends' stories were spun alongside mine those first months of the new year, and the stories helped me keep my bearings. Delicate, elegant, brown-eyed Nellie, the painter I'd known since she was in high school: twenty years later I'd been one of the few to notice at the opening of her first solo gallery show that she was also showing in another sense: she was pregnant for the first time. And then that January she called me to apologize for missing our rendezvous and explained that her water had burst and she'd had an emergency caesarian a few days before. The baby had been born two months early. She was in the intensive care unit but breathing on her own. She weighed two

moth without a mouth that has a few days to live and reproduce on stored energy.

pounds, two ounces. The brain of the average adult weighs three. What does it mean to be a whole human being smaller than a brain?

I went to visit the sudden arrival a few times when Nellie was there, but the first time I visited alone, walking through the high-ceilinged gallery of incubators I was told I must not look at. Nellie's daughter was at the far end of the big room, and en route I caught sidelong glances of tiny lean human beings of all colors in their fields of soft white bedding inside clear plastic bubbles. The babies were dreams someone somewhere else was having. They were half-written sentences. They were little flayed rabbits. They were technological triumphs, since a decade or two earlier most of them would not have survived, and their survival now was due to techniques, machines, drugs, and monumental human effort.

Some of the premature babies might have been covered in lanugo, the fine fur that we all have at that stage when we're usually still swimmers inside our mothers; some might have all their blood vessels visible beneath their translucent skin; some might have no eyelashes yet; some might be too young to cry; but I only glimpsed them in passing. Sometimes the sacred and the transgressive are indistinguishable as something you should not look at, and they all looked as though they were not yet made to be seen. Their fat, their cuteness, their familiarity, had not yet arrived, and some of them radiated tubes and monitoring wires.

The baby girl I had the right to look at was an astonishment, a reminder of what else the term *human being* covers, since we so often use that term as though it meant autonomous rational ambulatory people in their prime, not the newcomers or the

Other moths and butterflies also live brief lives without eating. And other moths

invalids or the otherworldly or the ancient. Nellie's daughter was too small to even breast-feed, and she was fed through a tube, but she was breathing on her own, and her mother went and held her bare skin to bare skin for several hours a day. In a picture from a few weeks after her birth, her fingers wrapped around her father's forefinger like yours around someone's arm.

What she thought and felt was almost unfathomable. We had all once been her, though most of us had been concealed from view for a lot longer. Nellie was fiercely devoted to her daughter and hardly concerned about the big scar of the C-section, though still a little shaky about an operation in which her guts had been laid aside on the table and there was a chance neither she nor her daughter would make it.

They made it, but Ann was embarked upon the long, slow process of not making it. Nellie was a decade younger than me; gracious, midwestern, genteel, fair-haired Ann was a decade older. She had had breast cancer twenty years before, been treated, had recurrences and more treatment, and finally the ticking bomb had exploded like a dandelion clock and sown the seeds of cancer in her spine and her brain. When the cancer in her brain was discovered, I got an e-mail from her friend and assistant that went out to just a handful of people.

Thereby I found out that I was apparently part of her inner circle or otherwise of significance and set about visiting her and baking her pies regularly. She liked pie a lot. After the pie was too tricky to eat there were the apricots in syrup, which her sister spoon-fed her. She declined gently, in stages, but her will was as ferocious as that of the two-pound girl, and the few weeks or

drink the tears of sleeping birds. Sadness always contains distance, spaciousness,

months she was given to live stretched into more than two years. There was more chemotherapy, a port into her skull to drain the fluid, a lot of monitoring, a lot of help, and not so much hope.

One of the curious things about illness and calamity is what you come to hope for and what you become grateful for. Ann's assistant wrote jubilantly at one point, "She got up out of her chair five times in a row when the therapist was there!" In my own case, I was grateful that I had only this brief tourist's visit to the country of the ill, that I had insurance that would mostly pay for it and means for the thousands more in bills, that I was being seen at one of the best medical centers anywhere, that I was going to skip chemotherapy and radiation, that my one scar would be undramatic and my treatment would presumably forestall the hard destiny consuming Ann. I never told her of my diagnosis; it was too late for that; and I kept visiting.

The last time she came to my house for tea, I set up chairs and a table on the landing two flights up the three flights of stairs to my apartment, and we had the first round while she rallied for the third story. Then she couldn't do anything so strenuous and just floated around her house and landed in various chairs or walked from steadying handhold to handhold. I wrote to a mutual friend that she was fading like a flower. She became less and less ordinary, if ordinary is the busy absorption with the practical and petty details of everyday life. Ann's abilities were ebbing and flowing and mostly ebbing all this time, but it was as though the casing was being worn away and the light inside shone more brightly.

The last several months or year she was in that saturated present of people who don't have so much past or future at their beck and call, and her own love and luminousness were increasingly

takes us away, while happiness at best brings us home to this very moment, this

evident. And then she began disappearing in stages, from speech, from walking, from most forms of doing, then in the end from eating, so that she didn't make much of a hill under the bedclothes. She'd always been something of an escape artist, a gracious self-effacing person who surrounded herself with people who liked the limelight.

It was typical of Ann that when she first became ill she made it an occasion to be an artist and to do something for the people around her. She was always turning the conversation away from herself, and the artwork she made in response to her breast cancer seemed to come from that reflex. It also asserted that she was not passive or defeated in the face of her illness. She tiled a hundred feet of wall in the entry lobby of a hospital building from floor to ceiling with big ceramic slabs glazed in soft colors. Each one had had a plant pressed into it, the plant's name inscribed, and then a cancer patient, survivor, or caregiver had graven a story directly into the clay, or Ann had copied a poem or a text into it. It was like an herbal, the old books of plant remedies, broken up and pasted to a wall, like a botanical collection that was also a collection of confessions, a murmuring you walked by on your way to meet your fate upstairs.

They were a companionable series of stories for patients, a reminder that they were not alone in that space where people rarely dared to inquire about anyone else's odyssey. I had known for many years about those tiles in the lobby near the garden she also revamped, because you passed them en route to various other departments, and when I became an oncology patient I discovered another wall of them in shades of green at the far end of the waiting room in which I was going to spend so much time that season.

very place, so perhaps they are the sentiments of the far and the near (though rage

Some of them endeavored to be uplifting. Others were unhappy, grisly, or frightened. There were stark words of witness and haikus and expressions of gratitude and fury in among the images of leaves and stalks and flowers that were actually indentations, depressions, absences, the traces the plants had left behind.

Others' woes can be used as reproaches and sometimes are: how dare you think about your own private suffering when wars are raging and children are being bombed? There is always someone whose suffering is greater than yours. The reproaches are often framed as though there is an economy of suffering, and of compassion, and you should measure yourself, price yourself, with the same sense of scarcity and finite resources that govern monetary economies, but there is no measure of either. In high doses suffering is boundless and incomparable and overwhelming. Though sometimes paying attention to others gives you perspective, and in suffering similar to your own you might find encouragement in knowing that you're not alone.

It was that loneliness that Ann's wall of tiles sought to mitigate, and mitigates still. More than two hundred thousand women a year are diagnosed with breast cancer in the United States alone; about half a million children are born prematurely in this country every year; more than five million Americans now have Alzheimer's disease; about forty-four thousand are diagnosed with some form of leukemia annually. There are armies, legions, empires of the ill, the frail, the failing; it is the dark side of the moon we call being human.

Illness mitigates solitude in another way in that it attacks any notion that you are separate, autonomous, and independent. You require bone marrow or blood from another; the care of experts

and fear arise from the proximity of the unwanted as well as the absence or

and of the people who love you. You are made ill by a mosquito or a virus or an unknown environmental toxin or by an aberrant gene you inherited or some exciting combination of these things. You cannot ignore that you are biological, mortal, and interdependent.

When you are well, your own body is a sealed country into which you need not explore far, but when you are unwell, there is no denying that you are made up of organs and fluids and chemistry and that the mechanisms by which your body operates are not invincible. You may have pains in places where the healthy person feels nothing, you may when injured see your own bones, or see X-rays and be reminded of death's skeleton under the flesh of life, you may be invaded, have parts of yourself removed, or tubes, shunts, devices, plates, and more added, your chemistry and hormones may be tinkered with, drugs administered. The system has been opened up and so has your awareness of it.

Ann continued making art as she went deeper and deeper into the country of illness for the last time. She made a series of drawings of lines across sheets of grid paper, and because her hand shook, the drawings became registers of tremors, like the lines traced by seismographs recording earthquakes, like the lines shown by medical monitoring equipment. An unsteady hand is usually considered to mean that you can't draw, but she made the shaking into a means of recording the little earthquakes of her being and an assertion that life and art would go on for a while anyway. And they did, trembling.

With the help of her assistant and her sister, she then made a final masterpiece, a vast wall map of white plaster topographical reliefs of islands. Each island was connected by fine red string

departure or threat of departure of the desired). Sadness and happiness—if those

reaching out to the other islands, like flight routes for planes or birds or neural pathways or blood vessels. Or conversations, affections, alignments. I think of that piece as an elegant assertion that everything is connected. Each of us is an island of sensations confined to the realm beneath our skin, but a great deal of migration and importing and exporting connects most of the islands to each other. It does if you can locate yourself in an archipelago or trace the lines to where they reach others and the lines whereby others touch you.

The night before surgery Sam and Kat took me out to dinner and then Kat went to rehearsal and Sam and I went to Ocean Beach late at night. On the firm wet sand at low tide your footprints register clearly before the waves come and devour all trace of passage. I like to see the long line we each leave behind, and I sometimes imagine my whole life that way, as though each step was a stitch, as though I was a needle leaving a trail of thread that sewed together the world as I went by, crisscrossing others' paths, quilting it all together in some way that matters even though it can hardly be traced. A meandering line sutures together the world in some new way, as though walking was sewing and sewing was telling a story and that story was your life.

A thread now most often means a line of conversation via e-mail or other electronic means, but thread must have been an even more compelling metaphor when most people witnessed or did the women's work that is spinning. It is a mesmerizing art, the spindle revolving below the strong thread that the fingers twist out of the mass of fiber held on an arm or a distaff. The gesture turns

are even useful words, because as the years have gone by I have wondered if we

the cloudy mass of fiber into lines with which the world can be tied together. Likewise the spinning wheel turns, cyclical time revolving to draw out the linear time of a thread. The verb *to spin* first meant just this act of making, then evolved to mean anything turning rapidly, and then it came to mean telling a tale.

Strands a few inches long twine together into a thread or yarn that can go forever, like words becoming stories. The fairy-tale heroines spin cobwebs, straw, nettles into whatever is necessary to survive. Scheherazade forestalls her death by telling a story that is like a thread that cannot be cut; she keeps spinning and spinning, incorporating new fragments, characters, incidents, into her unbroken, unbreakable narrative thread. Penelope at the other end of the story archive prevents her wedding to any one of her suitors by unweaving at night what she weaves by day on her father-in-law's funeral garment. By spinning, weaving, and unraveling, these women master time itself, and though master is a masculine word, this mastery is feminine.

Women were spinsters before the word became pejorative, when distaff meant the female side of the family. In Greek mythology, each human life is a thread that the three Moirae, or Fates, spin, measure, and cut. With Rumpelstilskin's help, the unnamed fairy-tale heroine spins straw into gold, but the wonder is that every spinner takes the amorphous mass before her and makes a thread appear, from which comes the stuff that contains the world, from a fishing net to a nightgown. She makes form out of formlessness, continuity out of fragments, narrative and meaning out of scattered incidents, for the storyteller is also a spinner or weaver and a story is a thread that meanders through our lives to

want other language for emotion, if we would rather speak of deep and shallow,

connect us each to each and to the purpose and meaning that appear like roads we must travel. As we did on that midnight walk on the beach, trailing footprints behind like stitches.

"The 'I' is a needle some find useful, though/the thread, of course, is shadow," writes Brenda Hillman in her poem "String Theory Sutra." The English and Latin word *suture* has the same root as Sanskrit *sutra* or Pali *sutta*. They both have to do with sewing. The sutras, the most sacred texts of Buddhism, were named for the fact that they were originally sewn. The flat blades of palm leaves were strung together by two lines of thread that tied together the stiff, narrow pages like accordion blinds. The books were copied by hand over and over again in that climate of decay. Thus leaf became book, and knowledge was held together and transmitted in a thread, a line, a lineage.

The term *sutra,* as in the Platform Sutra, the Heart Sutra, or the Lotus Sutra, generally means a teaching by the Buddha himself or one close to him, as distinguished from the scholarly and philosophical texts that piled up afterward. The word is said to have arisen from the actual sewing or binding of these old palm-leaf books, but it must have had some more metaphorical sense, as though the sutras' words and meanings run throughout all things and bind them together, as though the threads are paths you can follow and veins through which life flows.

When you take the precepts or are ordained in the Soto school of Zen Buddhism, you are given a piece of paper on which is written the lineage to which your name has just been added. Written and drawn, since the names are inscribed on a long red thread that loops back and forth so that so much lineage can fit on a single large sheet. It's a kind of family tree that traces the teachings

because the things that move people to tears are sometimes joyous and because the

from student to teacher and to the teacher's teacher and beyond, following the Japanese Soto Zen masters back to Dogen, who brought Soto Zen from China in the thirteenth century and tracing the Chinese ancestry back to the first Chinese ancestor, Bodhidharma in the fifth century, and then through the Indian teachers back to the Buddha himself (though some older parts of it must be mythological).

It's called the blood lineage, as though you had been sutured to a new family whose ties are as strong and red as blood, been sewn into a new set of associations, or given a transfusion. Or become the newest page of a book that continues to be written, or sewn. It's a way of saying that Buddhism is nothing more and nothing less than a conversation that has gone on from generation to generation, not by palm leaves but face-to-face, a thread of ideas and efforts unbroken over 2,500 years. It makes the recipient of the blood lineage only the latest stitch as the flashing needle keeps working its way through the fabric of this existence.

And I, if sutures are sutras, what was I going to be stitched to? I got up before dawn that morning to wash myself in the harsh disinfectant they'd given me, and another friend took me to the early morning appointment. I changed into the ugliest hospital gown I'd seen yet, a billowing sack with snaps all along the top and two clashing patterns in green and brown, put on the blue cap that covered my hair, and the white support hose meant to prevent blood clots during the long stillness of surgery. Then the anesthesiologists came in to see me.

I had been well prepared for surgery but little had been said about the other procedure I was to undergo, the instigation of numbness, stillness, amnesia, and oblivion by drugs injected and

attempts to ward off sadness so often ward off depth instead—by distraction, for

then inhaled through a tube put down my throat and a mask over my face after the intravenous ones had taken effect. The doctor or medical student slipped a curved needle into a vein in the crook of my left elbow, and the drugs began to do their work. The drugs they give you induce a retrograde amnesia, so I must have been conscious for a little while after that, but those minutes were erased from the record and the next few hours too.

Happily erased, since what must have transpired would be horrifying to witness and excruciating to feel. Before anesthesia, major surgery was unbearable. The effects of agony made it a last resort, not a routine procedure, and speed was a surgeon's chief virtue. Ether and other early anesthesias appeared as miraculous solutions to the problem of pain in surgery, though they exacted their own toll. Administered incorrectly they were fatal. The drugs and techniques have since been refined, but there are still consequences and aftereffects that can linger for months and occasional permanent damage.

The anesthesiologist sits at the head of the patient during surgery like the host at a table. While the surgeons' job is to change, the anesthesiologist's is to maintain, to monitor and manage heart rate, breathing, blood pressure, all of which he or she can control with the mix and rate of drugs, bringing consciousness down like a banked fire and then withdrawing the restraints as surgery finishes and allowing consciousness and the body's own regulatory processes to return. I felt that interruption for a long time afterward, as though I had lost the beats of the music, the steps of the dance, and was stumblingly trying to recapture them, these rhythms that were my own metabolism.

There was a continuity that was my breath since birth, and the

example. Certain kinds of beauty make people weep, the moments "when hope

anesthesiologist cut that, tied a knot in it, put me on monitors and respirators, then started a new thread, and while I was stopped, the continuity that was my skin was cut, and I was altered, and then sewn shut with thread and knots. There are a thousand stories in which someone falls asleep or wanders off to fairyland and comes back unchanged to find that years, decades, centuries, have passed, but surgical anesthesia is the opposite adventure: you go to sleep for what seems a moment, and when you wake up everything is the same except yourself. You have been severed from who you were when you went in and stitched to another destiny and body, saved or maimed or both.

Five hours or so after I'd gone under, I regained consciousness in the recovery room, or that's where my memory returned. I must have wanted to believe that I was not affected, because I had a brief phase of overcompensatory brightness, when I tried to entertain my Czech nurse and somehow aired the only phrase in that language I know, *Nic netra vecne,* a phrase I learned when it was scrawled on a bust of Stalin paraded through the streets as that country liberated itself from the Soviet bloc in 1989. *Nic netra vecne:* nothing lasts forever. The nurse corrected my pronunciation and ignored my vital signs. The phase in which I reached for some interview transcripts and notes as though I would resume working right away faded and I settled in to being exhausted. I was being cured of soldiering on endlessly: my job was now to be still, which had become almost easy at last.

People who loved me were there to greet me, and so were huge bouquets of flowers. When they had left to let me rest, I realized I couldn't get out of bed. My left arm had the long curving needle in it, so I couldn't bend or flex it to lift myself up; my right side and

and history rhyme," the arrival of the long-awaited, the revelation of a pattern in

arm were injured and tender; and a muscle that ran down my torso had somehow been tweaked, so that it hurt and I could not use my abdominal muscles to sit up as I usually did. Dusk came as I was immobilized in the room with the masses of flowers, without a call button or lights. I tried shouting for help to see what happened. Nothing did. Darkness fell.

The beautiful surgeon came in later, about a dozen hours into her workday to tell me that everything had gone well under her aegis and to see how I felt. She summoned the nurse and upbraided her for my blood-stained gown, my missing call button, my poorly arranged equipment, the uneaten tray of food in front of me. Then Dr. Pam came with her fiancée and some more appealing food, and I threw up even the delicate things I had requested, repeatedly. It felt as though my stomach had been sealed and my system had not woken up again, and so I took nothing in that night. Later, Mario the night nurse took my blood pressure and found that it was astonishingly low, since I had nothing to drink for almost twenty-four hours. He pumped fluid fast into my veins and woke me up every hour to check on me.

In the morning I endeavored to return to civilization, changing into the beautiful orchid silk pajamas brocaded with a pattern of phoenixes and dragons that I'd bought in Chinatown and Jane's old dove gray crepe de chine kimono whose long sleeves made a perfect receptacle for the wound drainage bulb I was going to have to secrete somewhere on my person for the next three weeks. It was stitched into me with black thread, a sign that I had been invaded and was now to be literally drained a little.

I also contained some temporary plastic tubing for drainage, some other manmade materials, and a small square of denatured

the universe that is also the revelation of your own power of making and

skin matrix stripped of its DNA. I was in a minor way now a Frankenstein's monster too, containing a fragment of another's body, stitched into another lineage, and the artisans had done their work well. Somewhere in the maze of the hospital some of what had been me not long before was being inspected by pathologists, a book for others to read under microscopes.

A few days after surgery I realized there was a disk stuck to my back—a spongy circle with a metal snap—where the monitors had gone. It was strange to feel that I was so alienated from my body that this thing like a leech had been on me for days—and then I found two more, and then several days after that one last disk. They were reminders that while I had been gone I had become an inert object that others maneuvered, altered, and monitored. I was no longer I, and my body was not my own but something absent, inert, alien, waiting.

There is a serenity in illness that takes away all the need to do and makes just being enough. In that state I've only been in before with severe flu, there is no boredom, no restlessness, not much thinking about what should be done or what has been done. You are elsewhere than consciousness, than everyday life, than the usual bodily awareness and social engagement. We call it doing nothing or resting: the conscious mind does little but the body works furiously, under cover of stillness, to rebuild, rewire, recharge. I recognized that this state must be some of what produced Ann's luminosity, though she deserved credit for some of it as a state of grace, not just depletion.

A major illness or injury is a rupture that invites you to rethink, to restart, to review what matters. It's a reminder that your time is finite and not to be wasted, and in breaking you from the past it

perceiving order, and sometimes just extraordinarily intense beauty, including

offers the possibility of starting fresh. An illness is many kinds of rupture from which you have to stitch back a storyline of where you're headed and what it means. Every illness is narrative. There are the epics, in which you will ultimately triumph over what afflicts you and return for a while to your illusory autonomy, and the tragedies, in which the illness will ultimately triumph over you and take you away into the unknown that is death, and the two are often impossible to tell apart until they resolve.

Then there are the enigmatic illnesses whose prognosis is uncertain, in which well-being comes and goes unpredictably, with the difficulty of a story without a plot, or with an unfathomable one. Doctors are forever being implored and pressured to read the future from the medical evidence in the present, to confirm the story, but early on they learn that the rules are rubbery: the near-thriving suddenly collapse, the person at death's door travels all the way back to rejoin the living, and the time line of death and likelihood of recovery remain unforeseeable.

I got better. Nellie's daughter got stronger and left the room of premature infants to go home. And Ann's end came. I visited her a week after my own surgery, taking the bus across town, and reading to her an essay of mine about Mexico and slowness and stories and snails, subjects I thought she might like even if she took in no more than the tone of voice and the attention. I talked to her about her own accomplishments and influence, and she beamed. The next visit I read her the "Garden of Live Flowers" chapter from *Through the Looking Glass*. I told her about the paradise of blooms her sister had coaxed into being in her own back garden and some of the ways she was like a flower.

I had been naive about how tenacious she was, and how long

moral beauties—justice done, truth honored, order or wholeness restored. Maybe

life can live in a body that is so racked and weakened. She would look into my eyes directly, with tenderness. There was so little sense of separation, or embarrassment that it was as if she was looking into the mirror, and perhaps to some extent she was. She was radiant for a while and then everything got worse. I went to see her when she was not conscious at all, but restless, vanishing, dreaming her way back into nonexistence.

And then, on a day of roaring, relentless winds that tore down branches and shingles and signs, she was gone. They asked me to write and deliver the elegy, and so I did in front of a few hundred people while I was still feeling frail myself. I said Ann's words, her friends', and my own for her, and a couple of days later I got on a plane for Iceland.

from that we can extract a definition of beauty that has more to do with depth:

8 · Unwound

What's your story? There are so many ways to tell it. When the near capsized like a ship, the far swept me up. I flew over the untrammeled lands of the subarctic and then across the sea. From the air Iceland looked like a high-relief puzzle of dark stone and pale vegetation and blue water. It was as strange as another planet. In the calm, sparsely populated airport, Fríða and the regal Klara were waiting with a big car to bring me and my bundles of books and warm clothes past long miles of knife-edged lava upholstered in thick moss to the city of Reykjavík. In the city I wandered dazed and jetlagged and still convalescent and contemplated pale people, a stuffed two-headed lamb in a store window, and the view north across the blue waters of the wide fjord to the sharp mountains still clad in snow.

Luxuries and fine goods had been scarce in Iceland's penurious past, but one shop on a side street had teetering stacks of fine china from not so many decades ago. The plates, cups, and saucers were all painted in the soft blue-gray of an overcast day and adorned with gulls. Even these bits of domesticity on which families had eaten their best dinners recalled the cold sea and the birds that travel such distances across it. Beyond the city and the one person I knew in this country, far away from everything, was my temporary home. A couple of days after landing, Klara drove me

beauty is one of the things that make you cry and so maybe beauty is always tied

there through hours of rough terrain with big rocks and occasionally tiny trees.

The Library of Water, which had formerly been a library of books, was on a hill overlooking a harbor on a small peninsula jutting north off a big one extending east. Beyond the harbor was a vast bay or fjord, this one scattered with nearly three thousand islands from the size of a room to the size of a farm. On the other side of the Breydisfjordur archipelago were the mountains of the Westfjords, Iceland's remotest reach, white with snow in those first days of May. Seabirds flew between the islands and nested on them in great groups, secure in this land in which the only native mammal is the rarely seen arctic fox, thought to have arrived on ice floes from Greenland. The small islands lack even foxes.

Writing about that archipelago now makes me think of my friend Ann's last installation, her white plaster islands mounted on a white wall and connected by a network of red strings, though for that scatter of small Icelandic islands only bird flights and the occasional boat trip must have connected each to each. Ann's piece made as she was dying was a map of everything, of connectedness itself, like the neurons of the brain and the veins of the body and the roads of the country. You can speak as though your life is a thread, a narrative unspooling in time, and a story is a thread, but each of us is an island from which countless threads extend out into the world.

I have pulled out one thread from the tangle or tapestry of that particular time, and nothing in my account is untrue, except perhaps the coherence of a story, when really there were many stories, or the heap of events and details and imperfect memories from which stories are spun. One thread led to New Orleans. One

up in tears. And maybe we can practice taxonomy, in this case of the things that

thread led to Iceland. One to a raft on the Grand Canyon a year later. Another led to Burma or at least to contemplating Burma. Five days after my breakup, the day I was invited to Iceland by Fríða's phone call, I went home and called my friend Marisa. That evening, the two of us organized a demonstration in support of the uprising led by Buddhist monks in Burma.

Three days earlier more than ten thousand monks had marched through Rangoon and thousands more had walked through at least two dozen other Burmese cities, risking everything in that land of absolute repression. The photographs of long lines of bare-armed shaven-headed men in deep red robes flowing through their cities brought tears to my eyes, as did the later images of legions of citizens lining the streets to protect them. I think of them now as like the red threads that connected Ann's plaster islands or as the new red blood cells that constantly flow forth from the white temples of our bones. They came out in defense of life and in doing so risked death, as did the smaller population of nuns in their pale rose-colored robes.

Most of us try to avoid trouble, danger, and death, and here was this unarmed multitude walking toward all three for the benefit of others and maybe for, as Buddhists like to say, the benefit of all beings. It was breathtaking, and it made you want to walk with them, made you breathe the air of those moments of emergency when the personal falls away and with it the usual fears and timidities. It made you wish to be brave and maybe it made you brave, since emotions are contagious. There were few risks for most of us elsewhere, but we could at least walk with them from afar and stand up for them.

In this isolated, devout nation that had been ruled by a military

produce tears rather than drink them. Pain. Sorrow. Loss. Thwartedness. Joy.

junta for almost half a century, there were said to be exactly the same number of monks and soldiers. The monks and nuns acted on behalf of the impoverished majority who had been racked by hardship when the government abruptly increased fuel prices that August, and on behalf of monks who had themselves been injured at a peaceful demonstration earlier in September. These were minor incidents in the major trouble that was life under a brutal dictatorship. They acted because it was time to act, because hope had arisen and change seemed possible, because they had a degree of immunity in that devout, superstitious country, because one of the core principles of Buddhism is the nonseparateness of all things.

But the monks had separated themselves from the military. They had at the height of the uprising performed the rare and extraordinary rite known in Pali as *patam nikkujjana kamma,* the overturning of the alms bowl so that nothing can be put in it. Early every morning Burmese monks circulated through the cities and towns, each carrying a dark bowl. They lived in the trust that the bowls would be filled, that they would manage to eat, and they tested it every morning. The test had mostly succeeded for millennia of South Asian monastic life. The daily rite proved you could live without certainty or money in a beautiful interdependence with the rest of society.

To give to them was to gain spiritual merit, so the act of giving went both ways in those transactions. The bowl was the site of an exchange of the spiritual for the material. Overturning the bowls banned the military and their families from giving alms, effectively excommunicating them and denying them other religious rites of passage. The monks marched through the streets holding their bowls upside down, a denunciation made scathingly public. To refuse to accept the gifts was to refuse to confer the reciprocal gifts, to break the threads that tied those secular people to monastic life and to the life of the spirit.

Whatever tiny contribution I may have made to that doomed uprising was more than recompensed by what it did for me. The monks in Burma and the supporters in my own city and all over the world constituted a community of dignity and principle that was a refuge for me at that particular moment. It was astonishingly beautiful, these unarmed people standing up to a dictatorship that would eventually spatter some of their blood on the walls of the monasteries, murder some, disappear some, drive others into exile or out of the temples, and silence many more. The ordinary people come to protect them in the streets in those hopeful days were braver yet.

Two days after Fríða had invited me to Iceland, Marisa and I managed to get a few hundred people to come to our city's Chinese consulate, China being a major backer of the regime. Many were Buddhists, most were wearing red, or donned red fabric brought by the famous Vipassana Buddhist teacher who was a committed organizer during that time. He had lived among the monks of Thailand and Burma and everything happening in the latter country was vivid and personal for him. I asked my muralist friend Mona Caron to draw the eyes of the Buddha as an elegant elaboration on that old chant "the whole world is watching." In pastel, on a piece of paper four feet high and eight feet wide, she made the eyes appear while Burmese émigré children watched, entranced, in front of the wall of the consulate.

They were huge, serene, sad, gorgeous, green, staring, and

and understanding. Arrival. Love. Mortality. Precision. Or maybe we can call

almost glaring, and where the third eye might be was a little image of the earth with Burma picked out in red. The curve of the earth hovered on the bottom edge, so that the eyes rose over the planet like burning green suns. The drawing, once I mounted it on heavier paper with sticks on either side, became the banner carried in the subsequent demonstrations. Marisa and I had moved faster than the established channels, and soon afterward the local Buddhist and Burmese communities began to organize together and we could draw back. But I never forgot that red river of monks circulating through the cities of Burma, and the connections that I made during that uprising lasted.

Mostly we tell the story of our lives, or mostly we're taught to tell it, as a quest to avoid suffering, though if your goal is a search for meaning, honor, experience, the same events may be victories or necessary steps. Then the personal matters; it's home; but you can travel in and out of it, rather than being marooned there. The leprosy specialist Paul Brand wrote, "Pain, along with its cousin touch, is distributed universally on the body, providing a sort of boundary of self" but empathy, solidarity, allegiance—the nerves that run out into the world—expand the self beyond its physical bounds.

The familiar fairy tales map only limited possibilities in the end. After all, they're mostly about getting—getting affluence, security, a spouse, offspring, the usual trappings. Even nowadays people who lack the full complement of these particular goods are reminded, subtly and not, that they should have them or that they have failed. The idea of a life lived by another pattern and measured

depth the genus and all these other things the species. Moths drink; birds sleep;

by another standard remains out of reach in these versions. What's your story? The goals matter. The foundation stone of Buddhism, the life of the Buddha himself, is a fairy tale run backward.

Twenty-five centuries ago, a man was born to aristocratic parents and walked out one night to become a seeker, a monk, and eventually a teacher, but we know only so much about this historical figure. The facts of his life were embroidered and embellished into the most perfect of anti–fairy tales, and that story is still with us, taught and reflected upon and retold all over the world. One version of the legend his life became was written down six centuries after his birth by a North Indian poet named Aśvaghosa. His epic poem, *The Buddhacarita,* or *Acts of the Buddha,* contains most of the incidents in the versions told since.

A rendition of the poem copied out about eight hundred years ago on fifty-five palm leaves still existed in a Kathmandu library in the last century—it's half of the original Sanskrit story. The rest only exists in Chinese and Tibetan translations. The book was literally a sutra, that word that first meant palm leaves sutured together and then meant the teachings of the Buddha. The words on that sutured, sundered book of leaves was translated into flowery English prose in 1894 and again in 1936.

In Aśvaghosa's *Buddhacarita,* all the legendary material is in full bloom: Siddhartha Gautama's mother's dream of a white elephant, his miraculous birth as his standing mother supported herself with a bough laden with flowers, his seven steps as he walked straight from his mother's womb and proclaimed, "I am born for supreme knowledge, for the welfare of the world—this is my last birth." That it's a story a little like that of the Christ

there are tears; there are dreams; there is difference. A mature insect, including a

child is a reminder that both belong in the fairy-tale category of the remarkable birth, from Peach Boy to Thumbelina.

Like Sleeping Beauty's parents, Siddhartha's father attempts to thwart the fortune told for him at birth, or one version of that fortune. The Brahman told him that his son would become either a great king who would rule the world or a great spiritual teacher. The father tries to avert the latter destiny by confining the prince to a paradise of gardens, dancing girls, banquets, and other sensual pleasures in which nothing appears that would provoke questions or quests.

The prince is born into what the fairy-tale goose girls and beggar boys arrive at in the end, the luxury that in the *Buddhacarita* includes golden elephants, golden deer, real deer pulling golden carriages, and strings of gems like garlands of flowers. Grown up into a handsome young man, Siddhartha marries a lovely woman and has a son and heir he names, bitterly it seems, Rahula, or fetter. The child further entraps him in the palace and the life his father chose for him.

Then the legend relates the crux of the story, how he goes out on roads his father has carefully stripped of "afflicted common folk . . . those whose limbs were maimed or senses defective, the aged, sick and the like, and the wretched" to spare him from pain and questions. The gods intervene. They send the four sights that are the pivot of this story, and the sights lead to the four noble truths that are the foundation of Buddhism. The first is an old man, and the sheltered prince's response is one of shocked dismay. He turns to his charioteer and friend for an explanation. This is old age, "the murderer of beauty, the ruin of vigor, the birthplace of sorrow, the grave of pleasure, the destroyer of memory," replies

moth or butterfly, is called an "imago"; the plural is "imagines," and the cells that

the charioteer, and adds that it is the fate of all who live long enough.

And then they meet a sick man, panting, with bloated belly and emaciated limbs, crying in pain and leaning on a companion for support, or a god in the form of such a man. The prince "trembled like the reflection of the moon on rippling water." They go out again on roads the king has cleared, and the gods send a corpse. The gods are impersonating the most dreaded and the least beautiful human conditions, with the clear premise that witnessing these states prompts us to wake up. The fourth sight doesn't occur in Aśvaghosa's *Buddhacarita* but does in many other versions: it's a *bhikku,* or ascetic wanderer, devoted to finding and addressing the cause of human suffering. Siddhartha Gautama turns away from his pleasures and toward the life of a bhikku.

It's hard to imagine a thoughtful person could remain literally oblivious of the facts of old age, sickness, and death, but most of us have a degree of obliviousness, willful or otherwise. We know the facts, but we don't always realize them with that imaginative, emotional engagement that makes them vivid forces and deciding factors. And then they do realize, or we do, or you do, and everything changes. I felt a little that way that apricot season when the drama of my mother's old age illness was quickly followed by my own medical adventure, Ann's slow dying, and Nellie's daughter's turbulent birth.

I've met privileged young people who were shocked when they discovered the destructive force of injustice in the lives of others around them. Some left their careers to work for human rights or to teach or to tend the damaged. Many lives have a moment of rupture that is an awakening and a change of direction. Another

bring about that maturity in moths and butterflies and other flyers are called

aristocratic firstborn son left his comfortable Buenos Aires life and a medical career because of one.

Ernesto "Che" Guevara was particularly affected by the unemployed miner and his wife shivering without blankets one night in the Chilean desert and by an old woman in Valparaiso dying of asthma and poverty. They were apparently not sent by the gods, but they woke him up and changed his life, and he took his own path, for better or worse, to end suffering. Siddhartha was twenty-nine when he left the palace to take up the life of a wandering ascetic, a seeker, a few years older than Che was when he got on the back of Granado's motorcycle and began the encounters that would change his life.

The moment when mortality, ephemerality, uncertainty, suffering, or the possibility of change arrives can split a life in two. Facts and ideas we might have heard a thousand times assume a vivid, urgent, felt reality. We knew them then, but they matter now. They are like guests that suddenly speak up and make demands upon us; sometimes they appear as guides, sometimes they just wreck what came before or shove us out the door. We answer them, when we answer, with how we lead our lives. Sometimes what begins as bad news prompts the true path of a life, a disruptive visitor that might be thanked only later. Most of us don't change until we have to, and crisis is often what obliges us to do so. Crises are often resolved only through a new identity and new purpose, whether it's that of a nation or a single human being.

I've envied the people whose lives suddenly rupture and afterward dedicate themselves wholeheartedly to a cause or a community. The new life seems the product of an urgent certainty that clears much of the ambiguities and ambivalences away. It was not,

"imaginal cells." These cells lie dormant in the larval creature and begin to

however, so simple for the prince. In one account he shaved his head and donned the robes of an ascetic as his family wept in the palace, but in the *Buddhacarita* he stole away in the night on his horse, cut off his long hair in the forest with his sword, and sent sword, hair, and horse back to the people he left behind without a farewell or an explanation. For the reader of fairy tales and Genesis, the startling thing is that he walks out of paradise of his own accord. Adam and Eve are driven out of paradise as punishment.

Buddhism takes change as a given and suffering as the inevitable consequence of attachment and then asks what you are going to do about it. Suffering, though, is not the most accurate translation of the Pali word *duḳḳha. Duḳḳha* means sky, ether, or hole, particularly an axle hole. Sukkha was a good axle hole for a wheel, while dukkha was a poor one, one that made the wheel wobble and bump, jolting the load. It could be translated as discord or disturbance, the antithesis of harmony or serenity. Everyone knows well that feeling of being out of tune, at odds, dissatisfied, anxious, full of dread, heartsore. Siddhartha said in his first sutra, the *Dhammacaḳḳappavattana,* "Birth is dukkha, aging is dukkha, death is dukkha; sorrow, lamentation, pain, grief, and despair are dukkha; association with the unbeloved is dukkha; separation from the loved is dukkha; not getting what is wanted is dukkha. In short, the five clinging-aggregates are dukkha."

Though many are drawn to Buddhism as a way to address their own suffering, the teachings emphasize care for others, compassion for all beings, as well as transforming the self who experiences pain, rather than extirpating the external causes of pain. These are ways of overcoming the attachment to self that is the experience of separateness. The Burmese monks were doing this

reinvent it in its mature form, its imago, when the caterpillar has dissolved itself work. They were doing it by performing the basic act of Buddhism, sitting still and paying attention to their breath, and by going out into the streets on behalf of the people of Burma.

Paying attention to your breath is about being present in the moment—I heard a formerly homeless woman who became a Buddhist priest say you do it so that you can be present enough to be compassionate toward others and not so caught up in your own drama. You sit still, count your breaths, watch the stories your mind makes arise, let them go, and maybe learn a little about your propensity to spin stories and the fact that you yourself make them. Even the absolute sufferings of the body can be regarded from various perspectives, though, for example, hunger or injury cannot be dismissed. Many of our emotional pains are yet more malleable, yet more responsive to perspective.

Zen priests and Burmese exiles and Buddhist teachers who'd spent time with the forest monks of Thailand and Burma were good company while I was thinking about stories, pain, and empathy. So was the photographer Subhankar Banerjee whose work I knew well before he wrote to me a few days before I left for Iceland. I wrote back, we corresponded, and we met a little less than a year later, at his house made of windows in New Mexico while it was snowing outside and steamily fragrant with Indian cooking inside, as if we were in two places at once, and perhaps he always was. An enthusiast with a head of unruly, wavy black hair who punctuated his narratives with laughs and with "Oh my God" when he exclaimed about how awful, wonderful, unexpected, or extreme something was, he was one of those people whose lives had ruptured and who had walked away from what

into a thick fluid and its old life is over; it's a death and resurrection at midlife.

was easy, safe, and lucrative. His empathy, however, was with a broader community than the human.

Born and raised in Calcutta, he had a great-uncle who painted and instilled a love of art in him when he was young, but an Indian youth with no particular means could not contemplate becoming an artist. He got an engineering degree instead and managed to enroll in a southern New Mexico university to study computer science and then physics. From there he went to do research at a national weapons laboratory, but Subhankar's real passion was outside his job.

When he arrived at the university in Las Cruces, he encountered a vast desert with few people. It gave him "the shock of space," he told me. "Because in Calcutta—you're lucky to have a square foot of space. But here I was in the middle of all this space and I didn't know what to do about that." He began exploring it; friends took him backpacking; he hated it; and then he was hooked, began camping, climbing mountains, became the outings coordinator for the local Sierra Club and then the vice chair. He started taking photographs, and after he had switched to a research job outside Seattle, he went on a commercial photographic expedition to Churchill, Manitoba, the easiest place to see polar bears, and photographed them.

In Churchill he made a photograph that has haunted him ever since. It shows one polar bear eating another. One creamy white bear stands up, its body pointing left and its head at center, small ears, black eyes, black nose, clean fur, its tongue out but a mild expression on its face. The other bear's head is at center too, its eyes shut, its fangs exposed, its head stained with blood, and its

The other meaning of the word imago *is an idealized image of a person, usually*

body torn open and partially gone, as much red meat as white fur on display.

What's disturbing about Subhankar's image is how much the two bears look alike, except for their expressions. It's an image not just of cannibalism but of a kind of narcissism, of devouring the self. You devour yourself because there is no one else you can reach. Though male bears kill others of their species and bears will feed on anything dead, there is an apparent rise in polar-bear cannibalism tied to the bears starving because the summer ice is failing.

Barry Lopez's *Arctic Dreams,* a disquisition on people, animals, ice, and light at far northern latitudes, is a lyrical book whose undercurrent of warning is more obvious today than when it was published in 1986. Climate change was an idea just being assembled by scientists at that moment; it would begin to enter the popular imagination a few years later. Lopez quoted an earlier traveler in Alaska, the Scottish-born American environmentalist John Muir, saying that polar bears move "as if the country had belonged to them always."

Though their country is both land and water—they are technically marine mammals—their survival depends on the expanse of sea ice on which they hunt. Or hunted. You could call them neither land nor sea but ice mammals. The ice is fragmented, vanishing sooner, appearing later, turning what was once the solid mass of the farthest north into open water. The country no longer belongs to them. At the end of his chapter on polar bears, Lopez describes seeing and touching an immobilized female polar bear about to be radio-collared "as though examining a museum specimen" and seeing her genitalia "in size and shape like a woman's.

a parent, formed early in life. As I was writing this I went to see my mother, and

I looked away. I felt I had invaded her privacy. For the remainder of the day I could not rid myself of this image of vulnerability."

Almost twenty years ago hermaphrodite polar bears began appearing, mutated and sterile. The changes that brought them closer to extinction were due to the chemical loads in their bodies, chemicals that had been swept north with currents and migratory creatures. And then came the drowning bears, bears trying to operate in a realm of summer ice that no longer quite existed. Mary Shelley imagined nature violated in isolated examples beyond which were the constants represented by the wild places and the order of things. She never imagined that all of us could become Dr. Frankenstein, chasing and fleeing our altered creation that is the landscape all around us and its invisible contaminants, everywhere, from within our bodies to the ends of the earth.

All these polar calamities represent a world that is itself monstrous, a manmade creation gone astray. It was part of what drew Subhankar to the arctic, this sense of need. He was thirty-three. He quickly quit his job, pulled out his savings, cashed in his pension plan, began talking to biologists, and made preparations to be gone a long time. He went forth into the utter unknown of the arctic winter and back to the artistic vocation he'd had as a boy.

Before long, he found the Inupiat hunter who'd become his mentor and guide, Robert Thompson, of the village of Kaktovik on Barter Island on the Beaufort Sea near the border between Alaska and the Yukon. Thompson taught him about cold and survival. They went to the Arctic National Wildlife Refuge to watch polar bears, this time not in a place where the bears were surrounded by viewers in tanklike cars, but where no other humans or settlements were near. The place had been photographed a lot

a little ways into trying to be with her in the era past, when she would murmur

in summer, but it was often described as an uninhabited wasteland in other seasons by those who wanted to ravage it, and Subhankar set out to show that this was not so.

Early on in their encampment, they saw a mother bear and her cubs play near their den, and he took photographs of the yellow-white creatures on snow so white that its shadows are pure blue. They look as though they are the only creatures in the world, one mother, two cubs, in the white world under a white sky, as though time has not been invented, as though the world has just begun, as though nothing can go wrong.

Hoping to photograph them again, Subhankar and Thompson stayed, and a blizzard caught them, and then another and another for twenty-nine days. The wind chill brought the temperature to 120 below. They were confined to their tent much of the time, where the winds made the fabric flap too loudly to talk much. Once the tent nearly got buried in snow. Many times they went out walking. "My benchmark is that, as long as I don't get separated from Robert, I won't die," Subhankar told me. In that environment, the wind and snow can obscure everything even a few feet away. "It's all white. You cannot have any sense of topography and up and down and hills and it just becomes whiteout and you really feel very scared."

"You couldn't see five feet in front of you and you could see the whole world," Subhankar recounted. "I went to the arctic, thinking that I'm going to a faraway place remote from my home country. As it happens, the arctic is connected. Today, after ten years, I call the arctic the most connected place on the planet. And that connection is both celebratory and tragic. It's celebratory because birds travel to the arctic from every part of the planet, including

more than an occasional word and I would only rarely understand it, I

from Calcutta. There is a species called the yellow wagtail that winters outside of Calcutta, where I'm originally from, and nests in the Arctic National Wildlife Refuge, where I've been working for ten years. So that's a celebratory connection."

It's tragic because of climate change and because of toxins migrating north along with the birds, the toxins that turned bears hermaphroditic and reach human beings as well. "Breast milk of Greenland women is now scientifically considered as hazardous waste," Subhankar said. "And that's because these toxins are migrating from all over the planet, and they're ending their migration in the Arctic. So all my work is actually a metaphor for this interconnectedness."

Subhankar made color photographs of the patterns of caribou herds seen from above, the trails made as they walk single file like quilting stitches across the white blanket of snow. Snow geese, in another image, form white dots on the golden tundra of summer cotton grass they fatten up on before they migrate south again. He often photographed from far away, not to distance himself, but to see the patterns the animals and the land made together. And sometimes he photographed close up, birds nesting, bones on beaches, hunters at work.

And then the work went far. It went to Washington, DC, when the fate of the Arctic National Wildlife Refuge was being debated. California senator Barbara Boxer held up Subhankar's newly published book of photographs to support her position against opening the refuge to oil corporations and drilling. The work was exhibited, reproduced, censored, became controversial, became part of the discussion, and Subhankar was committed, an activist on behalf of the circumpolar land, animals, and peoples.

remembered that I had a copy of Rilke's Duino Elegies *with me and read three*

Burma, India, Bolivia, Cuba, New Mexico, California, Siberia, Alaska, Iceland: the red threads connect the islands and the continents that are just larger islands. In between are the ideas and conversations that connect lives and minds, when they arise, when they work, when you pay attention, when you're lucky. I settled into my new home in Iceland, which was one room with a concrete floor and a bed, a table, and a chair, and two big windows that looked out onto the archipelago, where the arctic terns and the oystercatchers flew and the clouds came and went across the fjord that was punctuated with islands spreading into the distance.

Later in the summer I would go out a few times among the islands, and they held at least one revelation and many pleasures, but at first I just looked at them from the windows and from the harbor and from all the places I could walk to in this remote landscape into which I had been dropped. Late in the day the sun sometimes turned the sea silver like beaten metal and the islands black, though it was hard to say what was late when days lasted until midnight and after and darkness became scarce as summer advanced and night retreated. Each day was seven minutes longer than the one before, so almost an hour of night vanished each week, and the world around me became more and more suffused with strong cold northern light.

of them to her. In one of them were the words, "what we're now striving for was

9 · Breath

A long time ago on an active volcano in Central America, an old campesino called me over, showed me a small horizontal orifice in the earth like an open mouth, and urged me to put my hand in it. Steamy warmth was flowing out of it into the cool evening air. He told me, "The earth breathes." The age of most rocks is measured in millions of years, but the earth here was spitting up molten lava that glowed in the night and then turned into black lumps leavened with air bubbles, rocks a few minutes old and still hot from their birth.

A little smaller than Ireland, a little bigger than Cuba, Iceland is surrounded by thousands of tiny islands, alone and clustered on the coast and in the fjords like flocks of birds in the sky. It hangs like a big pale pendant off the theoretical necklace of the arctic circle, its northernmost point a small island named Grimsey just north of that circle, the southernmost point an even smaller island, one that appeared late in 1963. While much of the rest of the world was absorbed by news of the violent death of an American president, Icelanders were watching an island be born like a rough Venus, disgorged by a volcano beneath the sea.

They named it Surtsey, after a figure from Norse mythology, the fiery black giant who slays gods and sets the worlds on fire. The lava poured forth for another four years or so, when the island reached a square mile in size. Since then other natural

once / nearer and truer and attached to us / with infinite tenderness. Here all is

forces have gnawed it down to half the size it was then, and three satellite islets of volcanic ash appeared and disappeared in 1964–1965. As time passed, life assembled on the island. The first plant came less than two years after the mass appeared above the waves, and lichens came seven years into its existence, twenty species of plants in the first twenty years, of which ten faded away from the poor sandy soil.

"The most widespread species on Surtsey are sea sandwort, procumbent pearlwort, common mouse ear, annual meadow-grass, Poa annua and lyme grass," says an official report. Birds arrived. Gulls landed within weeks of the island's emergence, depositing the guano that built a richer soil. Fulmars and guillemots were the first to nest. Snow buntings and graylag geese came, almost ninety bird species in all, and twenty-one species of butterfly and moth. The first bush—a willow—came fifteen years after creation, and five years after the willows, seals were breeding on the young island. The descriptions make Surtsey sound like an orchestra, one instrument after another joining until there was the symphony that is an ecosystem.

Arriving in Iceland in spring, I watched the annual tuning up of the instruments everywhere as the earth woke up from winter. Mats of flattened gray plant stalks metamorphosed into grasses and great mounds of invasive Alaska lupine smeared whole hillsides violet. Tiny flowers appeared in clumps of greening moss on the stones that paved vast expanses of land. Bumblebees that seemed to have the lower levels of the air all to themselves were joined by tiny butterflies and other insects. New species of bird arrived and the patches of snow in the high places changed shape as they dwindled. As Surtsey gathered ingredients over the years,

distance / There it was breath. . . ." It was a good way to keep talking, and I

so this peninsula on the main island acquired its summer elements and sprang to life.

All of Iceland is new in geological time, an isolated mass sitting atop the earthquake-prone volcanic seam between the North American and European plates. It is not quite part of either continent, socially or ecologically, and the seam forms a magnificent rift valley of blue water in narrow stone chasms. It is so harsh, so new, and so remote that it has a simple ecology, with no reptiles and no native land mammals except the elusive foxes. A few species of rodent came with human beings over the centuries, as did reindeer and, most recently, mink. Iceland is a sanctuary and an empty quarter.

Volcanoes are still making and unmaking Iceland, along with other elemental forces in this place dominated by the nonbiological forces of heat, cold, wind, rain, rivers, ice, and snow. These are the forces that will flourish no matter what goes extinct, where the poisons migrate, and how the weather changes. The sun will rise, the winds will blow, the waves will lick the shore, the earth will tilt on its axis so that there is more light in summer, less in winter, rains and snows will fall, if not as they used to, and the waters will turn to solid ice and melt again. This is the world that existed before life and will exist after us.

In Iceland I lived under an homage to those primordial forces. The artist Roni Horn's Library of Water was a library of glacier melt, twenty-four floor-to-ceiling clear glass columns of water that had once been ice. In wintertime, Klara and others had gathered great chunks of the glaciers that covered ten percent of Iceland, and a different glacier's meltwater had been poured into each column. I slept under these glaciers, under the ice, and spare glacier

listened too, and the familiar lines became more fiercely elegiac, more stern and

melt sat in labeled five-gallon containers in the rear closet of my quarters. The map of where the ice was gathered showed a constellation of the frozen world of the *jökulls,* the glaciers, slowly melting: of Drangajökull, of Eyjafjallajökull, of Snaefellsjökull out at the tip of the peninsula, and the rest.

Upstairs, the irregularly spaced clear columns seemed to spell out another constellation or an archipelago in the oddly shaped room. The pillars of water from all over Iceland made the room Iceland in miniature and a memorial for what was not yet gone. You could see through the scattered columns, but whatever lay beyond became impossibly broad or thin or halved or twinned or vanished altogether. People became spires and balloons; straight lines bent; islands out the plate-glass windows warped; prismatic edges blurred all boundaries.

A friend who visited took a photograph of me through a pillar, smiling. In the picture, the far sides of my face are almost normal but in between lies a broad horizontal zone in which one central eye—the third, since there was also one on each side—was several inches wide above the broad balcony of my cheek. I was an island. My mouth was a pink channel that ran the whole length of the mass. It was me on the edges and an ebullient monster in the middle, with what looked like a few actual islands reflected in the broad expanse of my forehead. The distortion had pulled me apart as though a rift zone ran through me.

The Danish writer Hans Christian Andersen's fairy-tale masterpiece "The Snow Queen" opens with the tale of a distorting mirror made by a troll who is the Devil. The mirror shows the trolls their own ugly view of the world, and they fly up above the earth to force the angels to see themselves in it, but drop the

wild, spoken aloud. Moths drink the tears of sleeping birds. The contemporary

grinning mirror when they are en route, up high. It breaks into innumerable sharp fragments. The scattered splinters of glass find their way into people's eyes and make them see the world as the trolls see it, and some "even got a little piece of mirror in their heart, and then it was quite dreadful. The heart would turn into a lump of ice." It's a narcissist's and cynic's mirror that freezes the heart and distorts the world.

Glass, ice, mirrors, are all the same thing in this tale, cold, sharp, clear stuff. One of the mirror splinters finds its way into the eye and then the heart of a poor attic-dwelling child named Kai. He jeers at his companions, mocks his grandmother, and runs off to join the big boys. He is growing up out of the insularity of childhood, into self-consciousness, new cravings, and competition. The story is sentimental at its edges, fierce at its core, and full of snow. The boy's grandmother calls snowflakes "white bees," and he asks whether these bees have a queen.

When the Snow Queen comes to town, Kai hitches his sled to her sleigh and she pulls him out of the town, out of the warmth, out of the familiar, into a blizzard with snowflakes the size of "white hens" and then she brings him into the sleigh, wraps him in a bearskin, and draws him close. It's a terrifying seduction. "She kissed him on the forehead," says Andersen. "It was colder than ice; it went right to his heart, which was already half ice. He felt as if he would die, but only for a moment, and then he felt fine."

Roni Horn had collected Icelanders' stories about weather in a book meant as a companion piece to the Library of Water, a book called *Weather Reports You*. A postmistress named Margret Asgeirsdottir told of delivering mail in a blizzard when she was very young and of lying down in the snow and falling asleep.

poet Robert Hass once wrote of this most solitary of poets, this man who was

A bulldozer woke her up as she was freezing to death because she had fortuitously laid down in the center of things. "But walking in a snowstorm, you just feel tiredness coming on and, oh! it's so nice just to lie down in the soft snow."

Horn herself wrote of how weather itself is the dangerous beast in this otherwise mild island: "Weather with its apolitical, amoral, and wanton violence is murderous if you don't pay attention to it, murderous if you don't respect the magnitude of it. Weather moves rivers, and makes them too. Weather blows roads away or turns them into mud. Weather washes the rocks out of the mountains and dams the roads. In the interior, near the glacier, for example, the winds get so bad you crawl on the ground to get past them. You can't open your eyes, not even slits, because the fast air lashes them, lashes and burns like small sharp whips. Sandstorms stop visibility a foot in front of your face; this is a way of being lost without having gone anywhere. When the glaciers melt, just a little, the earth trembles to the gushing violence of engorged rivers. Water is picked out of the ocean and thrown in the air, whole fields of water are thrashed out of lakes. Statistics show weather is a leading cause of death on the island."

You could read "The Snow Queen" as a story about primordial forces versus animal empathies or even cold versus warmth. The boy with the ice in his heart, Kai, disappears into the north on his sled, and his friend Gerda, from the adjoining attic, misses him, weeps, waits for spring, kisses her grandmother good-bye, and walks to the river to begin looking for the boy. She gets into an oarless boat that isn't tied securely and the current carries her a long ways away. An old woman who is an enchantress pulls the boat to the bank and brings the girl to a cottage in a flower garden

always putting distance between himself and intimacy: "There are pleasures,

where all the year's flowers bloom at once, a garden outside time. She forgets her quest until she weeps and her tears water the earth so that a rosebush springs up and reminds her of the roses at home.

Tears are her magic; the roses wake her up to her task; months had passed, so she escapes into a landscape where autumn is spreading, and falls in with a talking crow, and then a prince and princess, and then a robber girl, who unties her captive reindeer for Gerda to ride. The talking reindeer, who is himself a marker of how far north she is, carries her deeper into the north, into the country of winter, into her quest. On his back she reaches the home of a second old woman, a Laplander who sends her on with an introduction written on a dried cod to a third, a Finnish woman further north. This third fate or fairy or crone lives almost naked in a hothouse and puts ice on the reindeer's head to keep it comfortable.

Even the reindeer implores the short grimy Finnish enchantress for aid for Gerda; it's a fairy tale in which everything helps the humble and openhearted, in which each creature, save for the trolls and the Snow Queen, serves the principle of warmth in its own way. But the Finnish woman replies, in this story of women and animals with hardly a man, "I can't give her any greater power than she already has. Don't you see how great it is? Don't you see how people and animals want to serve her, how she has come so far in the world in her bare feet?"

The reindeer takes her onward to the palace of the Snow Queen, where the frozen Kai is playing the Ice Game of Reason with flat shards of ice. If he can organize them into a pattern that spells out "eternity," he'll become free, but he never can. It's not

forms of nourishment perhaps that most people know and he did not. What he

reason or pattern but emotion that will free him, in the form of more tears from Gerda, whose grief makes him remember, so that he weeps out the speck of glass and is himself again. Weeping like ice melting, like winter snow turning into spring rivers, a spring that comes as grief, as waking up to suffering that is the beginning of doing something about it, weeping tears of affection and loss that are always hot and sometimes make roses grow.

In Blindman's Buff and Pin the Tail on the Donkey and piñata-smashing parties, the surrounding group directs the blindfolded child with the words warmer and cooler as she gets closer or farther from her destination (and it's the same in Spanish *"caliente, caliente, frío, frío"*). The goal in these games is to make contact, and coolness and distance are equated, as though the destination, the thing desired, were radiating heat. If you go far enough south toward the tropics, coolness is an ideal, as it is in Buddhism, the subtropical religion. There it represents calm, equanimity, the opposite of the heat of passion, of the burning world the Buddha talked about in his Fire Sutra soon after his enlightenment, the sermon that preaches that everything is burning.

The coolness of Buddhism isn't indifference but the distance one gains on emotions, the quiet place from which to regard the turbulence. From far away you see the pattern, the connections, and the thing as a whole, see all the islands and the routes between them. Up close it all dissolves into texture and incoherence and immersion, like a face going out of focus just before a kiss. Let me get some distance on it says a person begging for what we call perspective. Cool as in jazz cool: "marked by steady calmness and self-control," says a dictionary.

knew about was the place that the need for that nourishment came from. And he

The Buddhist nirvana, or paradise of the mind, comes from the word to blow out, as with a candle or flame; it's an extinguishing of the heat of passion; an exhaling breath, a letting go. The Buddha's key memory of childhood happiness under a roseapple tree is a memory of coolness; and he sits under another tree to achieve enlightenment. When the demon Mara comes with his armies to tempt and intimidate him away from this destiny, flinging storms and challenges at him, he asks the earth to bear witness for him, because he has no one else to ask. Stay cool. The earth roars, and the demon's army flees. It's a volcanic earth that speaks, that breathes, that roars, like the body affirming its existence against the phantasms of the mind.

Everything travels. Even the story of the Buddha came to Iceland several hundred years ago like a migratory bird, another fairy tale that mutated as it meandered. Boddhisattva became the Arabic Budhasaf or Yudhasaf, which became the Greek Iosaph and the European Joasaph, who was long revered as one of the two saints who converted India to Christianity. The story migrated from Syriac to Greek to Latin to a Norse translation of about 1250 that is credited to King Haakon the Younger, who may have done it himself or more likely commissioned it. An independent Icelandic translation from a German version was made a couple of centuries later.

Both tell the story of the prince whose father tried to protect him from the world and from knowledge of suffering, of how he finds it anyway, and goes on to a monastic life. "Thus it was," said a caustic writer in 1895, "that by virtue of the infallibility vouchsafed to the papacy in matters of faith and morals Buddha became a Christian saint." Which was viewed as problematic if you

knew how immensely difficult it is for us to inhabit that place, to be anything

wanted facts with untangled lineage, but if you prefer stories to migrate as freely as birds and mingle and evolve, it's a joy.

Stories migrate; meanings migrate; everything metamorphoses. Birds flew north in the summer, the golden plover from northern Europe to Iceland, the whooping swans from Scotland among other places, the tiny Icelandic wheatear from as far as northern Africa, but the arctic terns came all the way from the antarctic realms. I wandered around my temporary home on this island shaped like a heart, the volatile ice-covered heart that occasionally beat, with lava, boiling water, and steam in its veins. The farthest point I could reach on foot was Helgafell, the sugarloaf hill around which stories were wrapped like clouds, and where Gudrun Osvifursdottir was buried a thousand years before, the proud woman at the center of the Laxdaela Saga and all its slaughter and loss.

Once a farmer who spoke only Icelandic gave me a ride back from Helgafell in a rain; and cashiers spoke brusquely to me about money in the low-ceilinged, fluorescent-lit den that was the chain supermarket; and there was a librarian with some responsibility for the Library of Water who provided practical aid every now and again. Otherwise no one spoke to me because Iceland was not good at strangers or because I had landed in a small town far away from everything else that was nevertheless too much like the white suburb I had dedicated my life to escaping.

The town of Stykkisholmur had been a fishing village, but everything changes, and Iceland's small fishing-boat economy had been sold out to transnational trawlers. Everything migrates, but the old boats were mostly hauled up on land, their propellers full of dried seaweed and their windows checkered with fading

other than strangers to our own existence. To learn not to be a stranger is the

permit stickers from years before. Words travel, because the word *arctic* comes from *arktos,* Greek for bear. *Cancer* is Greek for crab. Memory, or one of its locations in the brain, the hippocampus, means seahorse. A bestiary is buried in our language.

The bears for which the arctic was named were traveling too, swimming long distances and floating away on the fractured summer ice, coming to Iceland and dying there, and running out of space or out of ice everywhere. That the locals were not good at visitors the two polar bears who came ashore that summer found out. The first one was thought to have swum two hundred miles from Greenland, though it may have come on drift ice some or most of the way.

"There was fog up in the hills and we took the decision to kill the bear before it could disappear into the fog," said the police spokesman for the north coast, and the environment minister said the bear was shot because the drugs to tranquilize it were nowhere to be found quickly, and the local veterinarian said he had those drugs in his car but not a gun with which to shoot a tranquilizer dart. The first polar bear to be recorded in Iceland arrived in 890, suggesting bears had been showing up before human beings had, but they never settled and bred and became resident as foxes and people did.

A second bear arrived a couple of weeks after the first, and this time Copenhagen zoologists were supposed to take it back to Greenland. Police shot it instead, as though it had been a criminal. A twelve-year-old girl had spotted it in front of her parents' farm on the north coast, white against black lava. It had been feasting on eider ducks' eggs, so perhaps it died happy, though the happiness of polar bears takes some imagining.

---

burden of the Duino Elegies." Moths drink the tears, and the elegies arrived in

---

I hardly felt welcomed in the town where the Library of Water was situated, but I didn't feel like a polar bear, a threat, just slightly nonexistent. Maybe like an elf. That summer, on the other side of the island, I met a drunk man in a bright muffler who began to tell me stories about the elves. Eve, he said, had several children, and one day God came to inspect them. She had been washing them, but she was embarrassed to show the grubby ones not yet washed, and so she hid them.

God, who seemed to be a fierce inquisitor, thundered, "I know all things. Do you think that I don't know how many children you have?" And he sentenced the hidden children to be hidden forever, to become the race of elves. They cannot be seen by ordinary mortals, though clairvoyants can see them. There might be, the drunk man added, twice as many people in this room as you think, and he gestured vaguely at the cavernous former slaughterhouse in which some art had been installed and some people were standing around, and maybe some elves.

In this former fishing village, actual fish were also as invisible as elves—the chain supermarket only sold frozen fish, along with fresh mangoes and avocados from ten thousand miles away—though some fresh fish must have been smuggled into the fish-processing plant on the outskirts of town. But the town still celebrated the national holiday of Fishermen's Day on June 1. That afternoon the ferry that docked twice a day on its journeys across the fjord was to take the townspeople on a free excursion and so I joined the crowd. We must have been out for hours, but no one looked at me and no one spoke to me even when lunch was served belowdecks and I sat at the same table as some of the locals.

Rilke's head like visitors from afar, Rilke a butterfly hunter trying to put himself

---

I thought of the expression "breaking the ice," but I had been quiet so long it was hard to break.

The boat sailed out past the harbor's blocky island and toward the islands father away. It was a fair day, with a pale blue sky full of soft white clouds, not sunny but clear. Off in the distance there was an island that looked, from the harbor, like a pyramid, the highest island in the archipelago. I had been looking at this island named Klakkeyjar a long time. We went past smaller islands that showed rough cliffs, green tops, a crowd of birds haloing each one like flies around a horse, and went onward.

As we swung around from its south to its west side the pyramid became two pyramids like a pair of breasts jutting up out of the sea. It was startling to realize that what I had seen for a month as one peak had always been two, and more startling was to see that these peaks so resembled human anatomy. When we drew nearer, I saw that they were not symmetrical in size or shape. And then the ship came so close that the peaks disappeared and we were alongside a dark stone cliff stained white with the excrement of birds who nested on its narrower ledges, while mosses and grasses grew on the wider ones.

Seen from above, Klakkeyjar didn't look like breasts or pyramids at all; with all its inlets, bays, and tiny peninsulas it was more intricate than a puzzle piece. Around A.D. 982 one of Klakkeyjar's bays had harbored the ship of the fugitive Eric the Red before he led Icelanders to settle Greenland. In summer people still gathered eiderdown from the eider ducks' nests, as they had for centuries, and pastured sheep on some of the larger islands of the Breidafjordur archipelago, and the bird refuge named Flatey was

in the way of strangeness, letting it feed at his tears. In 1912 he had been walking

still inhabited. The boat went back, the island turned back into the familiar pyramid, and I returned to the Library of Water.

I read, I lived in others' lives through books and letters, I wrote, often to friends about my own life and the life around me, I slept, I stretched, I thought about the past and future, I made meals from the strange ingredients available at the grim cavelike market I thought of as the troll den, I went walking out in the awakening landscape where the crying birds and shaggy, friendly horses seemed like the society to which I had been admitted. It was peaceful but strange.

Even earthquakes are the consequence of tensions built up over long spans of time, imperceptibly, incrementally. You don't notice the buildup, just the release. You see a sick person, an old person, a dying person, the sight sinks in, and somewhere down the road you change your life. In movies and novels, people change suddenly and permanently, which is convenient and dramatic but not much like life, where you gain distance on something, relapse, resolve, try again, and move along in stops, starts, and stutters. Change is mostly slow. In my life, there had been transformative events, and I'd had a few sudden illuminations and crises, crossed a rubicon or two, but mostly I'd had the incremental.

Director Walter Salles said of his Che Guevara movie, *The Motorcycle Diaries,* "I always thought of this film as if you were walking under gentle rain. After two hours of being exposed to it, you would be wet but without having felt the heavy, imposed dramatic effect of it." Zen teacher Shunryu Suzuki-Roshi said the same thing, more or less, about spiritual endeavors: "After you have practiced for a while, you will realize that it is not possible to make rapid, extraordinary progress. Even though you try very

on the cliffs near Duino Castle on the Adriatic when he heard the opening line

hard, the progress you make is always little by little. It is not like going out in a shower in which you know when you get wet. In a fog, you do not know you are getting wet, but as you keep walking you get wet little by little."

Sometimes I thought Iceland was a perfect place to convalesce, because it was as serene as the seaside cures Victorian doctors once prescribed. Sometimes it seemed like a terrible place to be stuck, because it was cold in so many ways. There I changed by degree, the terrible anxiety of the past year draining away, the peacefulness sinking in. The whole episode seems like a dream now, a long phase of floating along with sudden images flashing up. Maybe this ability to live in the insularity of a dream was as restorative as sleep.

I traveled a little, and on the south coast of Iceland had one magnificent midsummer day that began with a long walk on a path edged with tiny flowers past the largest glacier in Europe, went on to a bay in which the glacier was calving icebergs that were vivid blue in a blue inlet of the sea, and then traversed a long strand of wet sand that reflected the white clouds and blue sky so that heaven and earth were indistinguishable, and the clouds overhead seemed to be almost close enough to touch and those near the horizon seemed to be very near infinity. It was as close to a vision of paradise as I've been granted with my eyes open. After that I saw another bay full of hundreds of swans and a steep valley through which dozens of thin waterfalls trickled and poured from the heights. That day ended at a robin's nest Klara showed me in the low willows in the quiet light at midnight, five small mottled eggs like turquoise stones. But mostly I stayed home in the Library of Water and its locale.

addressed to the angel. He wrote the first elegy immediately, parts of others soon

After the expedition to the islands on Fishermen's Day, I went out twice more in the archipelago beyond the Library of Water. Once, a local man who'd worked on the open fishing boats in his youth took me, his half-English niece, and a stray American photography student out in a little boat called *Snót,* and we landed on Krakkeyjar. We drifted apart, wandered the rocky and boggy expanses of it, picked bilberries. The pyramid that had become breasts and then a puzzle piece was something else again up close. Another time I bought a ticket to go out on a sightseeing boat.

We passed by the Krakkeyjar island on the same route, so that the pyramid again turned into breasts, and then into cliffs for birds to nest on. Birdshit streaked down from the nests like white branches of a chandelier whose candles were eggs, whose flames had wings. On the way back the crew dragged the ocean floor and on a steel table on the deck dumped out a load of scallops, sea urchins, crabs, mussels, and starfish, bright like internal organs laid bare by surgery or butchery, the vivid color and life hidden under the surface of the sea.

Some of the other people on the boat gulped live scallops and cut open spiny urchins for their roe. I picked up a huge, heavy red starfish with thirteen arms that looked like the sun itself and threw it back into the sea, and it dipped further than did the actual sun during those midsummer days when night was a faintly dim phase that came for an hour or so long after midnight.

thereafter, and then "he needed to live with his desolation," Hass said. The poet

10 · Flight

In the bare room under the old library on the hill in the town at the tip of the small peninsula on the cold island so far from everything else, I lived among strangers and birds. The birds were mostly new species I got to know a little, the golden plovers plaintively dissembling in the grass to lead intruders away from their nests, the oystercatchers who flew overhead uttering unearthly oscillating cries, the coastal fulmars, skuas, and guillemots, and most particularly the arctic terns. I delighted in the impeccable whiteness of their feathers, the sharpness of their scimitar wings, the fierceness of their cries, and steepness of their dives.

Terns were once called sea swallows for their deeply forked tails and grace in the air, and in Latin, arctic terns were named *sterna paradisaea* by a pietist Danish cleric named Erik Pontoppidan, at the end of a turbulent career. He had lived part of his life in Norway, written a natural history of that land, made himself unpopular enough that he had to migrate back to Copenhagen, and there composed another monumental tome, an atlas of Denmark. In that era when the Swedish Linnaeus, like a second Adam, was naming all the plants and animals in Latin, new names were waiting to be invented for all the species on earth. Thus Pontoppidan gave several northern birds their scientific names, but it's not clear why in 1763 he called the black-capped, white-feathered arctic terns *sterna paradisaea:* birds—or terns—of paradise.

He could not have known about their extraordinary migration, back in the day when naturalists—and Pontoppidan himself in his book on Norway—thought swallows buried themselves in the mud in winter and hibernated, rather than imagining they and other birds flew far south to other climes. Of all living things, arctic terns migrate farthest and live in the most light and least darkness. They fly tens of thousands of miles a year as they relocate from farthest north to farthest south. When they are not nesting, they rarely touch ground and live almost constantly in flight, like albatrosses, like their cousins the sooty terns who roam above the equatorial seas for years at a time without touching down. Theirs is a paradise of endless light and endless effort. The lives of angels must be like this.

The far north is an unearthly earth, where much of what those of us in temperate zones were told is universal is not true. Everyone walks on water, which is a solid. In winter, you can build palaces out of it, or houses out of snow. Ice is blue. Snow insulates. Water crystallizes into floating mountains that destroy whatever collides with them. Many other things turn hard as rock in the cold. Nothing decays, and so time stops for the dead, if not the living. Cold is stability and warmth can be treacherous.

Trees dwindle; shrubs cling to the ground; and further north nothing remains of the plant kingdom but low grasses, diminutive flowers, mosses and lichens hidden beneath the snow part of the year; and nearly every species but the reindeer and some of the summer birds is carnivorous. In winter, light can seem to shine upward from the white ground more than from the dark sky

explosion of imaginative force. Long afterward, I sipped at Rilke's tears, I fed the

where the sun doesn't rise or rises for an hour or two a day. And at the poles themselves, there are not 365 days per year but one long night and one long stretch of light, and the sun rises once in the spring and sets once in the fall.

Their opposite is the equator, where every day and every night of the year is exactly twelve hours long. The further north or south you go, the longer summer days and winter nights get. In Iceland, each day of spring was several minutes longer than the one before, so that in May the days went from nearly seventeen to twenty hours long, and by mid-June the sunset is at midnight and sunrise before three A.M., but there is no true darkness, no night. The sun dipped low around midnight or after and there were spectacular sunsets that melted into sunrises, because the sun never went entirely away.

Reykjavík is at latitude 64 and Stykkisholmur at latitude 65, about as far north as Fairbanks, Alaska, and one degree south of the arctic circle. If you go farther north, to, say, the town of Longyearbyen in the Norwegian arctic at latitude 78, the sun rises in late April and stays above the horizon until nearly the end of August, when sunset finally comes—a few minutes before sunrise. There, winter is a night as long as that summer day, running from the end of October until the middle of February. The twenty-four-hour cycle of day and night we think of as normal and daily comes as a rush of rapidly changing days and nights, flickering like a strobe, between the great day and the great night that each lasts a thousand hours or more.

Long ago, I had read about the white nights of St. Petersburg in Russia, at only 59 degrees north, and I had once spent a couple of weeks in the Canadian wilderness at that latitude near midsummer,

sound of them and myself to my mother, and, perhaps, you have fed upon mine.

when night was just a blush of darkness that generally began and ended when I was asleep in my tent. I had always wanted to see the white nights farther north, but actually living through them was a little disorienting. Perhaps if you live through the long darkness, the superabundance of light makes more sense and the two balance each other. But to have the northern light without the darkness seemed askew, even if it was nothing compared to the life of an arctic tern. I had asked Fríða about it when I first met her, and she told me that for her the year was like a long day in which she was out in the world in the summer and was more interior, spatially and psychologically, in winter.

Sometimes during that summer when the sky was often gray but never black, I would think that a task had to be done before darkness and then realize that there would be no more darkness while I was there, and it didn't matter so much when I rose, when I slept, when I traveled. I could go strolling at three in the morning here on this island of few dangers and in June and July no absolute darkness. For me day and night were time itself, and I missed the rhythm and structure they provide. I missed stars. Darkness no longer shut me in: I shut light out to sleep. It was as though I had entered a landscape that itself never slept, never dreamed, that never let up the rational alertness of daytime, the light of interrogation and analysis.

The sensuality of night had never been so clear to me, darkness descending like velvet to wrap around you and enclose you in its black cocoon, to take you to your other self and others. "Because the night belongs to lovers," sang Patti Smith when I was young, but it's lovers that belong to the night, or rather the night that liberates them to live in the moment, in their skin, in each other.

Psyche spills a drop of oil on her love and to get back to him has to journey

Darkness is amorous, the darkness of passion, of your own unknowns rising to the surface, the darkness of interiors.

In darkness things merge, which might be how passion becomes love and how making love begets progeny of all natures and forms. Merging is dangerous, at least to the boundaries and definition of the self. Darkness is generative, and generation, biological and artistic both, requires this amorous engagement with the unknown, this entry into the realm where you do not quite know what you are doing and what will happen next. Creation is always in the dark because you can only do the work of making by not quite knowing what you're doing, by walking into darkness, not staying in the light. Ideas emerge from edges and shadows to arrive in the light, and though that's where they may be seen by others, that's not where they're born.

Darkness is a pejorative in English, and the term has often carried emotional, moral, and religious overtones as has its opposite: the children of light, snowy angels, fair maidens, and white knights. "Darkness cannot drive out darkness; only light can do that. Hate cannot drive out hate; only love can do that," said the dark-skinned Martin Luther King Jr., but sometimes love is darkness; sometimes the glare is what needs to be extinguished. Turn off the lights and come to bed.

When you spend time in the desert, you come to love shadow, shade, and darkness, the respite they give to the menacing blaze of day that burns you out and dries you up. Heat is the desert as predator, just as cold is the arctic's biggest animal. Desert light is fierce, and at midday it flattens everything into a harsh solid, but early and late in the day light is golden and every crevice and fold and protrusion of the landscape is thrown into the high relief of

through hell and to the ends of the earth. The route is rarely direct. Psyche's story

light and shadow. At those times day and night intertwine like dancers, like lovers, and shadows are as powerful a presence as the things that cast them, or more so, growing and growing until the sun disappears below the horizon and darkness spreads like water on the land.

There was only one dark place left in Iceland that summer, or so it seemed to me, and I went there again and again. Elín, who I had met for one meal when I first landed, who had given her mother my book after she had received it from Úlfur, the boy with the wolf's name who had died, was a young artist then but bold. She had made a labyrinth titled *Path*. In a big room in Iceland's National Gallery, with the help of two meticulous carpenters, she built a zigzag route of gypsum panels that gave off that material's dusty clean aroma. One person at a time entered *Path,* and a pair of watchers in the outer gallery monitored entries and exits and occasionally went in for a rescue, like lifeguards.

When you stepped in from the daylight and the door closed behind you, the space seemed to be absolutely dark and then your eyes adjusted to the faint, faint light. You could move forward when you were blind or wait until you could see, but placing a hand on one side of the walls helped you travel too. The path turned at sharp angles, so that you knew that you were being turned around and around, and you lost track of the distance that you were going. It felt as though it was a long way and a long time, and you were very alone.

The light that leaked through the intentional, careful cracks in the walls and ceiling was faintly lavender blue—it came from fluorescent tubes—and it streamed across the space in strange

itself wandered north from Italy and became the French tale of Beauty and the

ways. It was easy to believe that what was dark was solid, what was light was spaciousness into which you could move, but reality as you bumped into it was often the other way around, with open blackness and hard pale surfaces.

Your expectations reversed, you moved deeper into the labyrinth, knowing now that you did not know what was solid, what was space you could occupy, but would have to test it, over and over. *Path* was a space in which you perfected the art of not knowing where you were, of finding out one literal step at a time. Did the path fork? Or was there only one route? How far did it go? Was the way out the same as the way in? All this would have to be found with the hands, eyes, and feet as you traveled.

All the while a subtle deep bass thump like a heartbeat sounded. It reminded you that you were deep within, enclosed, contained, unborn. On you went, and on some more, unsure, unknowing, unseeing, twisting and turning. At the end the walls began to press together and it was as dark as it had been at that first moment you stepped in and closed the door behind yourself. And then you could go no farther. It seemed as though it ought to feel claustrophobic, but I found in it an embrace of darkness, a destination, a handmade night.

There and back again took me ten or fifteen minutes by the clock, but the time inside had no such quantifiable measure. It was time apart, symbolic time, a slow journey to the heart of the unknown and the unknowable. It became a significant journey, one that had danger, doubt, a plunge into the dark side. I kept coming back all summer, seven times in all, once for so long the attendants grew concerned. I felt at home there, more myself than

Beast, written by Gabrielle-Suzanne Barbot de Villeneuve in the eighteenth

anywhere else in Iceland, somehow. Jules Verne's novel about Iceland was called *Journey to the Center of the Earth,* and this felt like such a journey, or such a center.

A labyrinth is an ancient device that compresses a journey into a small space, winds up a path like thread on a spool. It contains beginning, confusion, perseverance, arrival, and return. There at last the metaphysical journey of your life and your actual movements are one and the same. You may wander, may learn that in order to get to your destination you must turn away from it, become lost, spin about, and then only after the way has become overwhelming and absorbing, arrive, having gone the great journey without having gone far on the ground.

In this it is the opposite of a maze, which has not one convoluted way but many ways and often no center, so that wandering has no cease or at least no definitive conclusion. A maze is a conversation; a labyrinth is an incantation or perhaps a prayer. In a labyrinth you're lost in that you don't know the twists and turns, but if you follow them you get there; and then you reverse your course.

The end of the journey through the labyrinth is not at the center, as is commonly supposed, but back at the threshold again: the beginning is also the real end. That is the home to which you return from the pilgrimage, the adventure. The unpraised edges and margins matter too, because it's not ultimately a journey of immersion but emergence. Ariadne gives Theseus a spool of red thread to help him escape the Labyrinth in Crete (which must have been a maze by our modern definitions). You unspool the thread on the journey to the center. Then you rewind to escape.

In this folding up of great distance into small space, the

century. Beauty's kindness and the water she pours upon the beast's dying body

labyrinth resembles two other manmade things: a spool of thread and the words and lines and pages of a book. Imagine all the sentences in this book as a single thread around the spool that is a book. Imagine that they could be unwound; that you could walk the line they make, or are walking it. Reading is also traveling, the eyes running along the length of an idea, which can be folded up into the compressed space of a book and unfolded within your imagination and your understanding.

All stories have this form, but fairy tales are often particularly labyrinthlike. Something happens, and just as to get from the periphery to the center of a labyrinth you twist and turn, turn away from the center, journey to the farthest reaches before you can reach your destination, so in a fairy tale you are interrupted, cursed, cast out, bereft, and in order to get back to the place you're in, have to go to the back of the north wind or the top of a glass mountain. The route is rarely direct, and it often ends in a return to the beginning point.

If *Path* was a book, it was about not knowing, about being lost, and about darkness, the darkness of the deep interior, a book you read with your feet. But it was wordless and so had the penurious privilege of visual art, of being able to invoke many meanings without being pinned down by the specificities of words. Too, it was the thing itself, not the representation of the thing. It was darkness, a convoluted route, a throbbing sound, faint zones of light, perceptual confusion. It was a space only revealed over time through motion.

Anatomists long ago named the windings of the inner ear, whose channels provide both hearing and balance, the labyrinth. The name suggests that if the labyrinth is the passage through

like a baptism or a flood of tears is what disenchants him and returns him to

which sound enters the mind, then we ourselves bodily enter labyrinths as though we were sounds on the way to being heard by some great unknown presence. To walk this path is to be heard, and to be heard is a great desire of the majority of us, but to be heard by whom, by what? To be a sound traveling toward the mind—is that another way to imagine this path, this journey, the unwinding of this thread?

Who hears you? Elín had heard me when she read me and then invited me to listen to her darkness. My book and her labyrinth were two exchanges in what had become a conversation. I pictured Alice going through the looking glass when I thought of the way that Elín and Fríða had pulled me through my book into their subarctic world, a journey that seemed to be completed by entering Elín's art so literally.

We live inside each other's thoughts and works. As I write, I sit in a building erected on a steep slope, so that what is the first floor uphill is the second floor downhill. Someone thought through the site and designed this structure specifically for this corner; someone cut the lumber in a forest up or down the coast; someone framed the structure, plastered the walls, laid the oak floorboards, the pipes, and the wires; someone designed and others made the chair I sit on, all of it long before I was born.

Long before that people established ideas about what houses and chairs should be like. I am in this moment hosted by anonymous craftspeople long gone, or rather by their ideas and labor, surrounded by more ghosts in the books in the room and other remnants of trees, the language I speak, the body I inhabit with the adaptations and limitations of innumerable ancestors running

human form. It's a classic fairy tale in which everything wants to return home to

through it, the city around me, the countless gestures, acts, devotions, that keep making the world.

I am, we each are, the inmost of an endless series of Russian dolls; you who read are now encased within a layer I built for you, or perhaps my stories are now inside you. We live as literally as that inside each other's thoughts and work, in this world that is being made all the time, by all of us, out of beliefs and acts, information and materials. Even in the wilderness your ideas of what is beautiful, what matters, and what constitutes pleasure shape your journey there as much as do your shoes and map also made by others.

A few decades ago, there was a lot of postmodern anxiety about the idea that every experience was mediated. The anxious believed that some pristine direct experience had fled, as though the mediation had not begun ten thousand years ago and more, as though it were not part of the world worth looking at and the companionship all around even when you are alone, as though there could be a world without thought, without culture, without language, as though you could be outside, and outside was a desirable place. The real question was the caliber of what was mediating experience, and how much you're cognizant of it.

With practice, you can pause the conversation, in your head and around you, but exiting it is not an option; it is you; and if you're lucky, you're it, participating in making this tangible and immaterial world around us and within you. You build yourself out of the materials at hand and those you seek out and choose, you build your beliefs, your alliances, your affections, your home, though some of us have far more latitude than others in all those

the familiar, to the human, to the happy. The journey in these tales is full circle,

things. You digest an idea or an ethic as though it was bread, and like bread it becomes part of you. Out of all this comes your contribution to the making of the world, your sentences in the ongoing interchange. The tragedy of the imprisoned, the unemployed, the disenfranchised, and the marginalized is to be silenced in this great ongoing conversation, this symphony that is another way to describe the world.

Part of the opacity of visual art for so many people is that each work of art functions as a statement in the long conversation of art making, responding to what has come before by expanding upon or critiquing or subverting it. To walk into an exhibition can be like walking into the middle of a conversation that doesn't make sense unless you know who's talking and what was said earlier or know the language that's being spoken, though some artworks speak directly and stand alone.

You could view Elín's *Path* as a young woman's answer to the great Light and Space artworks of the very male California artists James Turrell, Larry Bell, and Robert Irwin, who in the early 1970s began working directly with light itself as a medium. Their work was concerned with perception, illusion, and with sublime beauty, as well as with the expanding question of what art could be. A decade or two earlier painters had begun a shift from an emphasis on objects to one on processes, and the logical conclusion was an art of light, of gestures, of interventions in systems, of invitations to act and perceive. The dematerialization of the art object, my friend Lucy called this.

At its best, visual art is philosophy by other means and poetry without words. Visual art asks the grandest questions, about the most essential ingredients of existence: about time, space, percep-

but the story itself keeps traveling. In Norway a white bear who speaks with

tion, value, creation, identity, beauty. It makes mute objects speak, and it renews the elements of the world through the unexpected, or it situates the everyday in a way that asks us to wake up and notice. This kind of art raises fundamental questions about the act of making, about what it means, whom it is for, what happens in that engagement with materials and history and embodied imagination. I arrived in the realm of visual art in my early twenties, and it was a spacious arena in which to come of age, one that opened up the terrain in which I would travel to create and to converse. I was invited into the conversation, to speak and to listen, and to learn.

Who hears you? To have something to say is one thing; to have someone who hears it is another. To be heard literally is to have the vibrations of the air travel through the labyrinth of the listener's ear to the mind, but more must unfold in that darkness. You choose to hear what corresponds to your desires, needs, and interests, and there are dangers in a world that corresponds too well, with curating your life into a mirror that reflects only the comfortable and familiar, and dangers in the opposite direction as well. Listen carefully.

To hear is to let the sound wander all the way through the labyrinth of your ear; to listen is to travel the other way to meet it. It's not passive but active, this listening. It's as though you retell each story, translate it into the language particular to you, fit it into your cosmology so you can understand and respond, and thereby it becomes part of you. To empathize is to reach out to meet the data that comes through the labyrinths of the senses, to embrace it and incorporate it. To enter into, we say, as though another person's life was also a place you could travel to.

Kindness, compassion, generosity, are often talked about as

authority comes for the youngest daughter of a poor man, who gives her away to

though they're purely emotional virtues, but they are also and maybe first of all imaginative ones. You see someone get hurt—maybe they get insulted or they're just very tired—and you feel for them. You take the information your senses deliver and interpret it, often in terms of your own experience, until it becomes vivid to you. Or you work harder and study them to imagine the events you don't witness, the suffering that is not on the surface.

It's easier to imagine the experience of people most like you and nearest you—your best friend, the person who just slipped on the ice. Through imagination and representations—films, printed stories, secondhand accounts—you travel into the lives of people far away. This imaginative entering into is best at the particular, since you can imagine being the starving child but not the region of a million starving people. Sometimes, though, one person's story becomes the point of entry to larger territories.

This identification is almost instinctual in many circumstances. Even some animals do it; babies cry in sympathy with each other, or in distress at the sound of distress. Neurologists now talk about mirror neurons. You see something you crave, you feel something painful, and areas of your brain respond. You haven't only witnessed something but also translated it into your own experience; you have felt with and for that other. But to cry because someone cries or desire because someone desires is not quite to care about someone else. There are people whose response to the suffering of others is to become upset and demand consolation themselves.

Empathy means that you travel out of yourself a little or expand. It's really recognizing the reality of another's existence that constitutes the imaginative leap that is the birth of empathy, a word invented by a psychologist interested in visual art. The

provide for the rest of the family. She gets on the bear's back and the story opens

word is only slightly more than a century old, though the words sympathy, kindness, pity, compassion, fellow-feeling, and others covered the same general ground before Edward Titchener coined it in 1909. It was a translation of the German word *Einfuhlung,* or feeling into, as though the feeling itself reached out.

The root word is *path,* from the Greek word for passion or suffering, from which we also derive pathos and pathology and sympathy. It's a coincidence that *empathy* is built from a homonym for the Old English *path,* as in a trail. Or a dark labyrinth named *Path.* Empathy is a journey you travel, if you pay attention, if you care, if you desire to do so. Up close you witness suffering directly, though even then you may need words to know that this person has terrible pains in her joints or that one recently lost his home. Suffering far away reaches you through art, through images, recordings, and narratives; the information travels toward you and you meet it halfway, if you meet it.

In the bare room under the old library on the hill in the town at the tip of the small peninsula up near the arctic circle on the cold island so far from everything else, I lived among strangers and birds, under melted glaciers, inside others' acts of making and imagination, inside the reverie of a young woman's darkness and a species' life in endless light, in a lull in the ongoing conversations and at a vantage point from which I could map them. When I think back on it, I see myself the way you remember yourself in events of long ago, a small figure amid a rough landscape of glaciers, waterfalls, lava rocks, rain, clouds, birds, islands, and books. Always, just beyond all these things, was the silver sea, the lace border around all land like the silence around all sounds or the unknowns beyond all knowledge.

into a subarctic version of "Cupid and Psyche." The tale's title, "East of the Sun,

11 · Ice

Not the slender gray book with the Viking ship embossed on its cover. Not the deep blue one with the endpapers that map Greenland and the Canadian arctic. Nor the turquoise one with the Inuit faces on the wide spine. Nor the dark green one with white letters and a white polar bear printed on the coarse fabric cover. But the first English-language book, a thick one titled *Arctic Adventure,* bound in pale blue with an embossed blue dogsled and blue driver. This one tells the tale of what it means to live inside your own breath. A house made of exhalations, as though your body were spinning itself a shell, as though you blew a bubble that froze solid, with you inside.

The Danish-Jewish explorer Peter Freuchen was twenty years old his first winter in the arctic and bursting with vitality and enthusiasm for the other world he'd entered. He volunteered to stay alone on the edge of the ice sheet in Pustervig in northeastern Greenland for the duration of the dark winter of 1906–1907. A few other men were there at the beginning, in a stone and timber house built for the purpose, about nine feet by fifteen feet. Freuchen's task was to go out every day and take weather measurements on the mountain, which sounds easy enough until you factor in that it was dark most of that time and extraordinarily cold, and that the wolves that ate his seven dogs were deeply interested in him as well.

West of the Moon," comes from the vast distance she goes, helped by the winds, to

It was so cold that even inside his cabin, even with the small coal stove, the moisture in his breath condensed into ice on the walls and ceiling. He kept breathing. The house got smaller and smaller. Early on, he wrote, two men could not pass without brushing elbows. Eventually after he was alone and the coal—"the one factor that had kept the house from growing in upon me"—was gone, he threw out the stove to make more room inside. (He still had a spirit lamp for light and boiling water.) Before winter and his task ended and relief came, he was living inside an ice cave made of his own breath that hardly left him room to stretch out to sleep. Peter Freuchen, six foot seven, lived inside the cave of his breath.

Vanity of vanities, says the King James translation of Ecclesiastes, and the word that was translated as vanity was the Hebrew word *hevel*. It meant breath or vapor, or something as transient as a breath, as fleeting as vapor. Except in the arctic, where the vapor in Peter Freuchen's breath became a structure, so that you might have been able to take away the house the way builders take away the wooden form in which they cast concrete and leave the ice that was solidified breath.

It was as though in the stillness of a dark winter alone, he had disappeared inside himself. No one to hear him, to answer, to turn the experience into a story, or to tell stories to pass the time, just breath. When he went out to get snow to melt for water or to chart the weather on the mountain, he sang, badly, to keep the wolves at bay. Inside he got so lonely he developed friendships with the teakettle and pots and pans. It was a baptism by ice, and when it was over he was of the arctic, where he would spend the prime years of his life among the Inuit and have the adventures he spent

complete her ordeals. She travels on the wind, outwits trolls, and washes out of

the rest of his life recounting. His books about the north appeared in English and Danish from the 1920s until after his death in 1958.

I first encountered Freuchen when I was in Iceland, reading a more recent book that mentioned him in passing. The passage that struck me wasn't about Freuchen's beloved Greenland, but the far north of Canada that is now Nunavut, the indigenous-administered homeland. It was about a small band of Inuit travelers he met nearly a century ago: "Halfway there, the weather changed suddenly. Oddly, it wasn't the cold that nearly killed them, but heat. During the night their snow huts caved in and the frozen bits of skin, rotted meat and bones used to construct their sleds thawed and were eaten by the dogs. They had no food and no way to travel. After eating their dogs they began to starve. Atagutaluk then ate the bodies of her husband and children. When Peter met Atagutaluk she had since married the village leader. 'I got a new husband, and got with him three new children. They are all named for the dead ones that only served to keep me alive so they could be reborn.' "

It wasn't the cannibalism but the sled made of frozen scraps that fascinated me at first: cold as a kind of enchantment that turned flesh into solid structures, like the pumpkin turned into a coach in Cinderella, the fairy gold that turns back into leaves in the morning, like the frozen breath I read about when I went deeper into Freuchen's stories, and warmth the curse. When I went to the source, I found that the sled or sleds weren't just scraps, and neither bones nor rotten material was used. Frozen flesh and hide were occasional materials for sled building in a place far from trees and wood and a time of limited access to metals.

As Freuchen describes it, "First they soaked caribou skins in

his white shirt the three drops of hot tallow she had dripped onto him at the outset

water at the edge of the ice. Then they rolled them together and placed some ice blocks on top of the skins to make them freeze in the exact shape of sledge runners. For crossbars they used thin slices of meat that had been frozen by being placed on the smooth ice and large frozen salmon that they planed down somewhat with an ax. Thus they fashioned useable sledges, and off they went one day just after the sun had returned—a good time to start on the trip."

Freuchen's first account in his 1935 book *Arctic Adventure* was glib, but the story must have haunted him a little, because he told it twice more, and with each telling the meaning of the story changed. In a book of his published two decades later, the green-and-white *The Arctic Year,* he no longer singled her out for disparagement. This time the crisis that befell her and her traveling companions was something that could happen to anyone. He told a story of a similar terrible thaw that had overtaken his own party traveling in the arctic.

In this second account, a warm night wind had overtaken Atagutaluk's party during a spring journey across the interior of Baffin Island. The world around them thawed while they slept in an igloo, the sleds had disintegrated, and the dogs had "taken advantage of the feast the thaw provided for them." The sleds were gone, the harnesses and sealskin traces were gone, the provisions were gone, and deep soft snow fell and made travel impossible.

Months later, a friend of Freuchen's named Patloq, traveling with his wife, came across an igloo that seemed uninhabited, though the dogs were urgently curious about something inside it. The lack of footprints outside suggested no one was there, and when Patloq went in he saw "two absolutely unrecognizable

of her crisis. That what in classical Rome was the God of Love appears to be a

creatures. At first he thought that he had run up against some supernatural beings and decided to take flight, but then his wife encouraged him to look more closely at the mystery." Inside were two skeletons, barely alive. In his earlier account Freuchen had not mentioned that another woman had lingered in those desperate circumstances along with Atagutaluk.

The party had eaten the dogs, the skin clothes, and then the dead, and still they starved until only these two were left. Upon being rescued, the other woman gave in to her ravenous hunger and died of devouring more food than her starved system could handle. Atagutaluk disciplined herself, ate sparingly, and survived. And in this version she told Freuchen, "Oh, don't think too much about it. Now I have a new husband and with him I have four new children, so I don't owe anything to anybody!"

And then Freuchen told the story again. This time, being stranded was not something that could happen to anyone and he did not compare his experience with a perilous thaw to hers. It was about the bad old days before new technologies and communications arrived, and he seems to blame much of the trouble on the perishable sled, not the weather. He did not compare it to his own series of calamities and near-escapes in the far north. This time the party who left the Igloolik area were trading fox furs, heading for Ponds Inlet and the Hudson Bay Company trading post there, hundreds of miles almost due north. Freuchen describes them as stuck in a district with poor hunting, and said nothing about the snow that plays a crucial role in his second rendition.

The two women are rescued, and "Atagutaluk, who knew the art of self-control, lived to a ripe old age. It was she who told me of the whole tragedy. She saw that I was deeply shocked when she

polar bear in Norway suggests how far stories travel, and how little Psyche's

told of eating her husband and her three children. It is considered very impolite for an Eskimo to 'remove the smile from the face of a guest,' so Atagutaluk hastened to reassure me. She had found herself a new husband, she told me. And she had had a child with him and was the stepmother of his other two children, so she no longer had any debt to the 'Great Being.'"

Three children. Four children. One child and two stepchildren. To get wood for sleds in the first version. To go hunting in the next. To sell fox furs in the last. Because of the warm wind. Because of the lack of modern or at least wooden equipment. Because of deep snow. Because of bad hunting. In every version there's the mother who eats her children, as though time ran backward, as though what had emerged from her and fed upon her was to disappear into her again. Cannibalism in arctic emergencies is rare but not unheard of, among explorers as well as inhabitants, and it's both a terrible transgression and a strange communion, a human body feeding and sustaining another body.

Human bodies sustain other bodies in various ways—the fetus feeding upon the mother, sometimes depriving her bones of calcium and other nutrients if she's undernourished, the baby living on milk for months or years afterward, the starving person's body entering catabolysis, whereby it feeds on its fat and then its muscle until the wasting has gone so far the system begins to collapse. The modern world of blood transfusions and organ transplants has been referred to by one writer as noble cannibalism.

But there is now a global trade in kidneys. Donors from poor countries—Turkey, India, Romania, the Philippines—sell them to the wealthy, while Chinese executions of prisoners are sometimes conducted in such a way as to facilitate harvesting organs

spouse's identity matters. He is the perplexing beloved, the one who is unalike and

for sale. Done against the donors' wills, these transplants are cannibalism of the most ignoble sort, commercial cannibalism. In certain parts of India, selling a kidney to pay for a daughter's dowry has caught on, according to Nancy Scheper-Hughes, anthropologist and cofounder of Organs Watch, in her testimony to a United States congressional subcommittee.

In the 1980s and 1990s there was a widespread belief, a folktale of sorts, in Latin America that children there were being kidnapped by people from the United States to use as organ donors for their own children. People suspected of such activity were attacked and one woman beaten into a coma. It was not literally true, but it was true in a metaphorical sense: the well-being and even survival of Central and South American children was being sacrificed for profit in the global north. It turned the complicated machinations of international finance into something simple and shocking.

I am myself a cannibal in a roundabout way. I was patched up internally with AlloDerm regenerative tissue matrix, a small scrap of what had once been someone else's skin, presumably donated, then sterilized, stripped of its DNA, and turned into an expensive brand-name product. We divide up the world as though there were real borders rather than delicately shaded degrees between the crazy and the sane, the good and the destructive, and I think of cannibalism as also a matter of degree. To what extent, in which ways, are you a cannibal, and how careful are you about who you consume? We consume each other in a thousand ways, some of them joys, some of them crimes and nightmares.

And if we consume each other in stories, then there are an abundance of stories of cannibalistic consumption, Kronos and

unaccountable and unaccounted for. He is what is lost that must be recovered to

Tantalus, Sleeping Beauty's stepmother, Hansel and Gretel eating a bit of a house made of food and facing being treated as food in return by its owner. In the German fairy tale "The Juniper Tree," the stepmother cooks the son and feeds him to his father, though he is miraculously reconstituted from his bones and birdsong to live again and revenge himself. Cannibalism and resurrection often go together.

Part of the transgression in Frankenstein is the recycling of corpses and their resurrection or reanimation by the doctor playing both God and grave robber. Atagutaluk resurrected herself by feeding on human corpses, a transgression by which she set herself apart from the rest of her people—she had to live alone for a year before she could fully return to her community. We are all resurrected in a way by food every day; we live off life, plant or animal. And one of the unmentionable facts of everyday life is that we're all made out of meat, as I remember when I walk alone, regularly, in the territory of mountain lions. The carnivorous Inuit sometimes say, "The great peril of our existence lies in the fact that our diet consists entirely of souls," which doesn't lessen the trauma of anthropophagi, of eating human flesh, but deepens that of everyday consumption of other sentient beings.

There's a version of an Inuit story that's been making the rounds in recent decades as "Skeleton Woman." A father throws his daughter into the sea, where the sea creatures devour her until nothing but a restless skeleton is left. Or a woman marries a handsome stranger who turns out to be a bear and she follows him under the ice where he's at home and she drowns. The underwater creatures nibble away all her flesh and leave a living skeleton. In

be made whole. The white bear is charismatic, an animal by day, a man by night, some versions a fisherman catches the skeleton and hauls it out of the sea; in others she wakes up in her home.

Young men run away from her. An old man comes and sings and drums the flesh back on her bones. It is told as a story of the emotional self withered and starved away and then resurrected by kindness and attention, a therapeutic story like "The Juniper Tree," in which catastrophe is wholly overcome and bodily resurrection is possible, where time runs backward as well as forward, what is suffered can be undone. Even death retreats so that the chance at happiness is given twice.

The story of Skeleton Woman bears a family resemblance to the many versions of the story of the genesis of the arctic sea goddess Sedna, the principal or one of the principal deities of the western arctic. Her story is as varied as Atagutaluk's, though since it's an ancient creation myth, not a report on a century-old calamity, the variations are less vexing. It's about a woman who would not marry. In some versions her father in fury wed her to a dog. Or it's about a woman who went off with what looked like a handsome man who turned out to be a raven. Often the husband she ends up with is a fulmar, a seabird that looks like a gull but is more closely related to shearwaters, petrels, and albatrosses.

In the version Atagutaluk's husband told one of his children, the woman married a fulmar, though people nearby had it that the woman was married to a storm petrel. The dog, the raven, the petrel, the fulmar is a cold husband. In the version Atagutaluk's great-granddaughter Alexina Kublu tells from the stories her father heard from his grandfather, "kipinngullakpak&unilu, ugguaqtualuugalualiq&unilu." That is, "she was extremely lonely,

and you wonder if the old tellers of the tale noted that in the far north he might

and very regretful." In all the versions of the story, the father takes the daughter back in his kayak and the abandoned husband pursues them with strong wind and turbulent waters. The small craft begins to capsize.

The father, never very kind to begin with, throws the daughter overboard and when she tries to climb back in, he chops off her fingers. "As the parts that were chopped off fell into the water, they became the sea-mammals," recites Kublu. "There now were seals, and square-flippers [bearded seals], and beluga. But because the woman whom they called Takannaaluk [the horrible one down there] had no fingers she wasn't able to [use a] comb, and so her hair became tangled. Whenever her hair got tangled, sea-mammals became entangled in it."

When the animals that were once her fingers got tangled in her hair, they did not swim up where the hunters could get them. People went hungry. When this happened, a ritual was held; everyone gathered in an igloo; the shaman was tied up, the lights extinguished; and he began to sing in the darkness. Eventually he went under the sea to comb her hair and restore hunters' access to the game. Freuchen went to one such ritual in Greenland, and he describes an agonized, ecstatic, frenzied, writhing group of people inside a great igloo, drumming, singing, and a shaman who despite being tightly bound disappears bodily and then after darkness is restored, returns. The light is lit; Freuchen sees him there sweating, exhausted, and the shaman says with what seems to be standard Inuit diffidence, "Just lies and tricks. The wisdom of our ancestors is not in me. Don't believe in any of it!"

In the skeleton story, time runs backward and things are restored to what they were before; the woman lives and gains a

be animal all the time in the long light of summer and mostly human during

kinder lover. What is broken can be mended, but what was human remains human, what was personal remains personal. In the story of the goddess of the sea, the heroine's needs are not met, but the walruses and seals are created, and the needs of the humans who tell her tale are addressed instead. It's not a fairy tale in which the wants of the individual are paramount. Damage and death are not undone, her fingers do not return to her body as flesh returned to the skeleton's bones, but out of them comes life and sustenance.

Atagutaluk's story is more like Sedna, in that the terrible things that happened are not undone, but she generated more life. Or it's more like Skeleton Woman because she became a skeleton near death and was then brought back to life. She was loved, was valued, was respected for surviving, because of the bounty that came from her. It's a story with some of the resonance of a myth, and it seems as if of events from long ago, from the dreamtime and the heroic age, though Atagutaluk's grandchildren are online and old acquaintances are on videotape.

To tell a story is always to translate the raw material into a specific shape, to select out of the boundless potential facts those that seem salient. Maybe Freuchen spoke too soon. Or maybe he mistook Atagutaluk's reluctance to distress a guest for blitheness about her ordeal. He seems to have even gotten the date wrong, because all other sources date the events not to 1921, as he does in his *Book of the Eskimos,* but to 1905. The woman who survived was very young, at the beginning of a long life with many more episodes to come.

No one ever stopped telling the story of the woman who survived somewhere near Igloolik after a terrible thaw in 1905. Freuchen didn't name the wife of his friend Patloq, or Palluq, who

winter's long nights. These marriages to animals are pervasive in the pattern that

discovered the starving woman or women. Patloq's wife was named Tagurnaaq, and she told the story herself, powerfully, with the sense of tragedy and oration of a great dramatist or a saga-teller, to Freuchen's traveling companion, the part Greenlandic-Inuit explorer Knud Rasmussen. Tagurnaaq's version begins with her husband, who had the gift of prophetic dreams, dreaming of one of his friends being eaten by his nearest kin. They were out traveling, and their sledge kept getting stuck all day, which she viewed as ominous. They arrived at a country of deep snow.

"Then we heard a noise. We could not make out what it was; sometimes it sounded like a dying animal in pain, and then again like human voices in the distance. As we came nearer, we could hear human words, but could not at first make out the meaning, for the voice seemed to come from a great way off. Words that did not sound like real words, and a voice that was powerless and cracked. We listened and kept on listening, trying to make out one word from another, and at last we understood what it was that was being said. The voice broke down between the words, but what it was trying to say was this: 'I am not one who can live any longer among my fellows; for I have eaten my nearest of kin.'

"Yes, we came to that shelter, and looking in, we saw a human being squatting down inside, a poor woman, her face turned piteously towards us. Her eyes were all bloodshot, from weeping, so greatly had she suffered. Palluq and I looked at each other, and could not understand that she was still alive and breathing. There was nothing of her but bones and dry skin, there seemed indeed hardly to be a drop of blood in all her body, and she had not even much clothing left, having eaten a great deal of that, both the sleeves and all the lower part of her outer furs."

you can trace through so many stories, mostly male animals and female human

The skeleton spoke: "'I have eaten your fellow-singer from the feasting, him with whom you used to sing when we were gathered in the great house at a feast.' My husband was so moved at the sight of this living skeleton, which had once been a young woman, that it was long before he knew what to answer. At last he said: 'You had the will to live, therefore you live.'" In this telling, her fathomless distress comes through as it does not in Freuchen's versions.

The story recalls extermination camp narratives of extreme starvation, of how it warped and weakened the mind, made food an obsessive thought, drove the body like a demonic force, made the sufferer into something other than his or her ordinary self. Possessed by emptiness, Atagutaluk had starved alongside the frozen corpses of her family, she told Patloq and Tagurnaaq, and then one morning when the sun came out and a little warmth was in the air, the desire to live seized hold of her. "It was much worse than dying. . . . It could not hurt the dead, she knew, for their souls were long since in the land of the dead." In this version there is no one with her; and her solitude is part of her suffering.

Patloq and Tagurnaaq, the couple who rescued her, had a daughter who says she too was on that grim expedition. Many decades later, she told a harsher version of the story than her mother and charged Atagutaluk with killing the other survivor. She describes the same kind of omens, the halting journey, a white partridge that called to them, and then she describes Atagutaluk as "a horrid sight! She was like a bird in its egg. She seemed to have a beak and some sort of miserable small wings because she no longer had sleeves." She had eaten them. "She was the very image of an embryo in the egg."

beings, including the arctic sea goddess stories in which a woman marries a dog,

Atagutaluk's family told the story too. The story changed, and changed, and changed again. They went out in summer, not winter. There were no children with them. They were hunting caribou. The husband instructed her to eat him, his flesh a willing gift, like organ donation, like the sacrifice of Christ, like the story of the Buddha who took the form of a rabbit and leaped into the fire to feed his hungry guest.

Rose Ukkumaluk, a woman who knew Atagutaluk, told the story as she remembered it to a video camera fifteen years or so ago. Grief and empathy come through as she speaks in her own language with subtitles, her old woman's voice grave and a little gravely. In this version, Atagutaluk survives alone, and there are no sleds or thaws. Ukkumaluk says, "She used to tell people to eat whatever was available. I used to eat with her. She also fed my children."

Atagutaluk's great-niece Apphia Agalakti Awa, who was born about a decade after Freuchen came through the region, remembers her well. "She was the one who handed out the meat. If people were hungry, if they didn't have any food, she would split her food with those people and make sure they had some of whatever she had. She would make up little teas, little sugars, she would share with all the people in her camp and give them each a little something. She didn't want anybody to be poor. . . . She didn't want anybody to ever be hungry and she made sure that everybody got the food they needed. That is how she became a leader."

No one died as a result of her actions, and many people lived. She was a benefactor to her own second crop of children, but also to the community. Baptized a Catholic in 1931, she took the name of Saint Augustine's mother, Monica. She became an emissary

a fulmar, a storm petrel, or a handsome stranger who turns out to be bear rather

between the white Christian world and her own people. This might be why she became known as "Monica Atagutaluk, the queen of Igloolik." She wore an actual copper crown of sorts, a band that went under her braids, and in the best available photograph of her, also holds a cigarette in the corner of her mouth rather jauntily. The caption on a photograph of her in one of the volumes of Rasmussen's *Report of the Fifth Thule Expedition* says that the crown was made from the band around a telescope's tube.

Both the elementary and the high school in Igloolik are named after her, so she is a strong presence now. The people who knew her saw a long and rich life with a brief, terrible incident early on. Freuchen saw only a corner of the picture. The picture always gets bigger; there is always more to tell; one thread is tangled up with all the others; even when it stops, other threads carry the story onward, beyond the horizon. Though which version was true I do not know: sometimes I think Freuchen got an earlier version before the embroideries and enhancements entered in; sometimes I think Atagutaluk's kin were better listeners.

I had begun by being fascinated with a sled that may not have existed, and certainly did not exist as it was described in the contemporary account I read first in that room in Iceland. I kept reading, bought Freuchen's books, was drawn by him into his cheerful version of the arctic, learned a lot, became enchanted by him, then disenchanted, found his three versions, went further, found several others, found in the end that much of the story fell apart like that sled. Beyond it was a remarkable woman whose life was only accessible in the most general outlines. She was stranded, suffered, survived, begat, sustained, was remembered with gratitude and admiration. It was a life.

than human. A Tlingit version of the story of the woman who married a bear was

Freuchen nearly died of a sled that did not melt, not far from where Atagutaluk lived. He was traveling in the Igloolik region in the early spring of 1923, when he went out alone to pick up cached supplies and got stranded in a blizzard. He dug a hollow, covered it with his laden sled, and crawled in to spend the night with the skin of a bear's head for a pillow and a sealskin to cover the entrance. Later, in the darkness he found that the sealskin would not budge—ice and a snowdrift had accumulated over it—and he was buried in a small, very cold space.

At a loss for a tool he shat, fashioned a tool from his own excrement, waited the little while it took to freeze solid, and then used it to chip away at the ice. Finally, he used his lungs, emptied and filled, to heave the heavy sled away, inch by inch, breath by breath. Outside at last, he could only crawl, and he crawled for three hours to where the others were. One of his feet had frozen solid, and he lost it, and he describes the pain, the gangrene, and the nightmares.

It's a gruesome story in which he inhales his way out of a cave even more confining than the one he exhaled into being at the beginning of his life in the arctic. He continued traveling in the arctic and elsewhere, joined the Danish Resistance against the Nazis, worked on movies, wrote memoirs of his adventures and novels, but nothing ever compared to his youth in the Arctic. He had two children by his first wife, a Greenlandic-Inuit woman who died of influenza in 1921, and his grandson, Peter Freuchen Ittinuar, was the first Inuit person to become a member of parliament in Canada, not so many decades ago.

There are stories that close in on you like the ice of his solidified exhales in that little house in eastern Greenland, stories you

told by a blind old woman named Maria Johns to an anthropologist named

escape with inglorious tools and inhales, as he did the cavern under the sled, stories that fall apart on you like the melting sled that might not have ever existed, stories that help you navigate in storms and the dark, as the stories of others' lives often do. The versions of Atagutaluk's tale say as much about the tellers as their putative subject.

Though it was a vision of coldness and whiteness that drew me north, I found there the darkness inside a labyrinth and stories of warmth, including the story of a sled that melted, a story that itself became a labyrinth that had at its center questions about how to tell and how to listen.

Catherine McClellan on July 16, 1948, near Whitehorse in Yukon Territory. The

12 · Mirrors

There is a man who has been reading a book for more than five hundred years. He holds it open so that individual pages are splayed out, separated from each other. The big book requires both of his hands to hold it, and his head is bent down to study the pages, so his whole body inclines toward his reading, the way a mother's body curves around a child. The book is not wide open but open enough to search through, and so perhaps the reader has been searching for a passage for half a millennium. That the book is pure white and wordless doesn't matter, for his robes are white, and his hands, and in the pale face that looks upon the pages the eyes are pure white too. Or rather a warm creamy color that is alabaster after centuries of exposure, like a white dress after a long journey.

The reader is one of forty surviving figures of mourners from the tomb of Jean Sans-Peur, John the Fearless, the duke of Burgundy (other figures were lost or destroyed during the French Revolution). They mourn a grasping man who died in 1419 and whom no one has mourned in earnest since before the stone was quarried from which they took shape, though the Carthusian monks at the Charterhouse the Burgundian dukes established prayed for their souls as a matter of course. Surely the artists who carved the figures were happy at the chance to practice their art at its fullest and highest expression. It is themselves they've made

husband sometimes has the form of a man, sometimes a bear, and the wife

immortal, their ability to speak fluently in stone, so that the material can say cloth or flesh or hair, can say sadness or contemplation or strength.

The small mourners—they're each about the height of my forearm—were exhibited in my city, and I went to see them repeatedly, thinking about my mother, about the chapter to be written, wondering about the draw of that whiteness, which was the whiteness that first captured my imagination in the Frankenstein footage of the man and his creation chasing each other across the ice. White like this, the color of mourning in much of Asia, is a kind of peace that is a little fatal, a little stark, the white of bones without flesh, of deserts, of the poles and cold, of the page without the words. It's the landscape of beyond, of before, and of after.

There is a joy in writing about or painting or sculpting pain or loss, the pleasure of seeing into the life of things is one of the least celebrated and most important of the panoply of satisfactions. These tomb figures whose broad faces suggest kinship or a single model and whose draperies are simple and flowing all convey something about the nature of stone, of gravity, of emotion, and though they are supposed to be grieving they seem instead to feel the solemnity of death. Some of them are actually reading, the only employment other than marching in procession that the mourners' figures have.

The several blank books for alabaster eyes are there to tell ours that the readers and mourners have access to a story—probably the religious story at the center of life in the late Middle Ages. The here always exists in reference to the there, the there in this case that is bound up in books—handwritten in those days on vellum, the skins of calves, so that a large book was a herd of animals

becomes a bear in the end and is obliged to murder her family after her brothers

transformed, in our era printed on wood-pulp paper in vast numbers so that softwood forests are laid up in the libraries for those who have eyes to see. Vellum lasts longer.

The centuries have not done much to the alabaster reader. I often wonder at the endurance of the inanimate. The stylish suit in which my mother got married is dark blue, with white piping and strong lines. With its shoulder pads and jaunty cuffs that come to angular points, it looks like a naval uniform, and like a uniform it made its wearer look more formidable, much more so than the faintly rumpled army khaki and cap my drafted father was wearing at their city hall wedding. In their military uniforms they began twenty years together in which he won most of the battles, though she won the war. Or they both lost the struggle for love and subsided into war. Or won it, since they begat four more people to continue the experiments. But the man she married has been dead a quarter century; the woman who wore that suit has not fit into it in nearly half a century.

Human beings have come in and out of existence, metamorphosed, declined, and the excellent midnight blue wool serge is virtually the same as it was more than five decades ago. She wore it with a white fur muff in place of a bouquet since the wedding was in winter, and the animal pelt was a ferocious substitute for flowers. The tall slender dark-haired young woman who wore it is now stooped over, an ancient whose hair is whiter than the statues of the mourners, whiter than milk, white as snow.

Even memory of that day is gone; no one else who was there is yet alive; but the photographs show them as they were, everyone young, hale, ignorant about what the next half century would bring them. The photographs have curled a little but they are

have killed her husband and driven her to her animal nature. The story explains

otherwise unchanged and unfaded. The pale pansy of her face under a jaunty little veil: if I could have warned her, I might have canceled my own existence.

The wedding ring she wore, gold with tiny round turquoises like the sugar jimmies that go on cakes and cookies, vanished long ago, but the gold must still exist even if the muff fell apart or was thrown away. Things that never lived don't die, and even the objects made out of the living—the paper from trees, the vellum from calves—can last for centuries. We wear out. The wool suit threatens to outlive everyone who knows or cares about it. And it is only wool and silk. Stone, metal, wood are far more enduring.

The whiteness of the page before it is written on and after it is erased is and is not the same white, and the silence before a word is spoken and after is and is not the same silence. Snow falls before and after the growing season; the era of my harmonious relationship with my mother flourished before my memory begins and after hers faded. She was herself being erased, a page returned to whiteness on its way to nonbeing, and as she went her hair blazed a shining white as light as snow or cumulus clouds.

She had long told a happy story, undoubtedly true, in which she wanted to have four children and did, and another one, equally true, in which she wanted to be independent, educated, emancipated, adventurous, and was full of bitterness and regret that all this had not transpired as she had imagined it. It had, in fact, mostly taken place, within the limits of her timidities, for she was fearful as well as furious and maybe the latter because of the former. She added up her life over and over, but the sums were never quite the same. Whose are? It's like measuring your shadow.

She seemed unable to hear me for so many long years but I

the kinship between humans and bears and the taboos on eating grizzlies, though

spoke elsewhere; I wrote; I became someone else, someone audible, I filled up pages, trees fell for my books. I never heard her describe a dream, and I don't know what she dreamed of. Did she know herself in this way I didn't know her? What were some of the other stories of who she was? Could she have told it another way, and would that have given her another life? I can take this other self of hers on faith, because there are depths everywhere, but I didn't come into contact with it much and wonder if she did.

Ours was a game of chess in which she had made the first move and from there everything went forward. Or at least certain moves were made possible. And others impossible, or at least unimaginable then. It's always easy for outsiders to instruct one on what should've been done—directions for being fearless or saintly are likewise easy to issue, a little harder to execute. Like chess, there are rules, and breaking them takes momentum or confidence or a vision of other ways of doing things or all those things at once. Knights fell, pawns crawled, decades passed, then finally the chessboard went white, the pieces lost their names, the game came to a halt.

There's a chess set by the conceptual artist Yoko Ono in which all the chess pieces and the board are white, like those mourners five hundred years before. The two arrays of pieces mirror each other: the army at war with itself. Or not. Ono's was an artwork about the cold war but also about the way you can erase the very notion that there are two sides and merge, and surely we two who were so alike could have been one side. Or were. Sometimes people endeavored to play chess, that game of medieval warfare, with Ono's pieces anyway, struggling to keep track of whose piece was whose, so that the game resembled one of those autoimmune

it's more than that. It's not a circular tale; nothing comes back to where it started;

disorders in which the body attacks itself. The monochromatic set called for another game, one in which there was only collaboration or contemplation or that other kind of play that is anarchic, with improvised and evolving rules.

Finally, the war ended. She forgot the stories that fueled her wrath, and when they were gone, everything was different. When I was in my thirties and things with her were at their worst, I'd considered never seeing her again, walking away from the chessboard. I think quitting then would've frozen our relationship at its worst point. In this late era, well down the road labeled Alzheimer's, my mother lit up at the sight of me. I wryly said to one of my brothers at this juncture, "It's like we're in the same family." It wasn't just that she was more pleasant for me to be around; she seemed to be more pleasant for herself. She had achieved something of the state people strive for through spiritual practice: a lack of attachment to the past and future and a wholehearted participation in the present. It had come as part of a catastrophic terminal illness, not a devotional pursuit, but it came.

There was an era in which my mother was a happy child. Perhaps there had been another one before my time. When that season came around again, the autumn after the apricots, it was hard to tell what caused it. I had put her on medications to calm her conduct and soothe her agitation, but it may not have been the medications. She had a degenerative brain disease that was rearranging her memory and her personality.

Whatever the cause, she lost her stories. They seemed to go quite suddenly—at least the stories about me. Nearly all the grudges, comparisons, expectations, resentments, ancient histories

what is animal remains animal and what is human goes away, and yet because

and anxious anticipations seemed to disappear in that second spring of her life when she seemed to have lost as many bad as good things and achieved a new equilibrium and a new joy. Occasional odd things surfaced. But mostly she was festive, even if her jokes that I was her mother had an edge—as well as an edge of confusion about how this world was organized and how we were related. With Alzheimer's time runs backward, and given that, maybe I was her mother, and certainly I sometimes played a mother's part.

Liberated from the burden of her past, things became incomparable, each slice of cake the most delicious cake ever, each flower the most beautiful flower. She took pleasure in a great many things in the life that she was leading as a resident in a dementia facility and was often almost giddy with enthusiasm. Sometimes she spoke of how terrible the disease of Alzheimer's was, but mostly she didn't bring it up and seemed unconcerned and unselfconscious about her condition and circumstance.

There must have been terror and dismay but I didn't see much of it and showing up and steadying her ability to function must have reassured her even if we didn't go to the heart of the matter. I grew adept in handing her back her information about what she'd done, where she was, who she'd been and who she was connected to, without breaking the surface of ordinary conversation, got used to covering the same ground repeatedly with aplomb, and eventually became competent at mostly one-sided conversations that weren't too off balance.

She was living in a safe place with assistance and attention always hovering, with art and music and exercise programs and meals and more help as her condition advanced. The caregivers

of these journeys without return, a kinship arises. A skinned bear looks

were mostly immigrants, and in her early days there she often advanced a theory that emotional warmth could be equated to the warmth of one's country of origin. It was not a very tactful notion, but the mostly brown- and black-skinned people who worked there were infinitely patient and kind. It was, in one light, a gracious bedlam and in another a place staffed by hosts of angels and saints performing miracles for the benefit of the disintegrating beings in their charge.

She clung for the first year or so to a black-and-chrome radio about the size and shape of a large book, which she hid behind her bed for fear someone would steal it and listened to up close, sometimes holding it almost as though it were a pet or an amulet. Perhaps she hoped the radio would pour back into her some of the information that was leaking away. And then the radio was swept away in the journey downstream and was no longer part of her life. I remembered it with a pang myself, a pang that she changed so fast and that I myself adjusted without always remembering that she had been someone else not long before.

Occasionally I'd realize that her condition would have been shocking if it had arrived suddenly, but she traveled so slowly it often seemed imperceptible until we reached another milestone. During the early stages, she felt more like a parent than she ever had, in that she was affectionate and enthused about me. She was also a child who needed help with many things. And everything was vanishing, more or less literally. She was increasingly impaired not in her eyesight but in her brain's ability to interpret what her eyes saw, an effect of Alzheimer's called "agnosia," or not-knowing. She told me early on that she recognized people by their voices,

terrifyingly human, a fanged and muscular man who never was. Moths feed on

not their faces. Faces were gone. Reading had vanished long before.

She could not tell a change in the color of the pavement from a hole in the ground, or a carpet pattern from objects she might trip over, so she became a tentative walker, and we took to holding her hand or her arm when we walked her. It was impossible to know what remained visible. She often could not see what was waved in front of her face or set before her on the table, but once when one of her nieces had come to visit and was walking with us, she noticed a geranium petal on the ground and exclaimed over it. I was surprised she saw that tiny scrap of pink after months and years of hardly recognizing anything and picked it up for her.

For a while I would take her to an Italian restaurant in a shopping plaza where the staff was indulgent about the eccentricities of our dining. She thought their salads were the best salads ever and enjoyed the excursions. On one such outing, she wanted a lipstick; she often did in that era. I bought them regularly and they vanished regularly. We went to the plaza's drugstore, and I tried to show her some shades of pink. She didn't seem to see them even when I waved them under her eyes, so I handed the uncapped lipstick to her and cautioned her that she couldn't try it on but should look at it.

I hoped she'd be able to see it if she held it. She attempted to try it on, I wrested it from her as gently as I could, and then we went through the same routine with a better shade of pink. Now it's obvious that it didn't matter what shade I bought; the goal was to have a lipstick because a lipstick signified something. But it seemed like respect to treat her like a woman who'd want to select

the tears of sleeping birds; we feed on the tales of loss and generation. The

her lipstick color with care. We ate our ravioli and salad without any further misadventures. Probably shortly thereafter the lipstick vanished. Not so long after that she forgot about lipstick.

My mother became different people, one after another, in the years after that apricot summer. She was a happy child for a couple of years. Then the precarious balance shifted, and she had more trouble with everything. It resembled in some ways the stages of childhood running in reverse, and as with a child, whatever arrangements suited her at a given stage didn't necessarily work when the next one arrived. How and when it would arrive was never clear in advance. Another thing to come to terms with was that there was no preventing or changing the course of events: the disease was a road she was going to go down no matter what. All we could do was help her travel it as gracefully as possible and locate what pleasures and comforts were available along the way.

There was an era in which my mother fell down regularly. Or at least the staff at the place where she lived thought she was falling down a lot. They would find her sitting or lying on the carpet and their protocol required calling an ambulance. They'd call one of us too. We'd rush over and try to ward off the emergency medical technicians' inclination to strap her to a bodyboard, to put her in an ambulance, to strip her and put her in hospital gowns, once to even catheterize her for a urine sample, to generally traumatize her when she had not been traumatized before they arrived.

A few times she had a minor bruise or scrape that might have been falling-related, but she was never seriously injured in this phase. I came to think that perhaps some of the time she was sitting or lying down. She was losing her ability to navigate, her balance, and her confidence. Her kind doctor proposed that her

California poet Gary Snyder retells Johns's tale in his essay "The Woman Who

caregivers were negligent in not preventing her from falling down, but there was no way to do so without depriving her of her liberty.

There were pretty grounds at her residence, with a rose garden and lemon trees, a pomegranate tree, primroses in front of the administration building, and other greenery, and a series of paths that let us take a fifteen-minute-or-so walk at her slow pace in the phase after walking around the neighborhood was over, long after I stopped taking her out into the confusing world of restaurant meals and car trips. She couldn't smell the roses—the disease had stripped that away early—but there was a porch-style swing near them we sat on, and the fresh air and walks were good.

One time we went across the little central street as usual toward the sidewalk on the far side and I tried to steer her to a curb cut. She wanted to go straight toward the curb instead and I helped her step up to the grassy higher ground. On the grass she paused a moment, then lay down calmly, almost gracefully. She had managed the step but not the adjustment in balance afterward, and this voluntary crumple was apparently her way of eliminating the risk of falling. Once she was down she was a little upset to be lying on the grass. She cried out, however, when I pulled on her arms to try to lift her, and didn't have any capacity to get herself up.

This was in the era when the drugs seemed to be making her gain weight, before the era when I eliminated the no-longer-necessary drugs, which came a while before she lost her appetite and began to grow frail and thin. I tried a few things and then sat down on the grass to keep her company, took my cell phone out, and asked the dementia facility to send help. She lay and I sat on the grass, becalmed. After a few more minutes, the imposing woman in charge that day came out to help us, and so did two

Married a Bear" and wrote his undergraduate honors thesis on another northwest

older men out on a stroll of their own. The three of them got her to her feet and she said to all of them or some of us or no one in particular, "I love you all."

One Thanksgiving holiday during this phase my brothers persuaded and helped her up the short flight of stairs to my middle brother's house. During the afternoon, too many people tried to help her and talk to her at once, and she got upset and overwhelmed. When it was time for her to go, my patient younger brother walked her to the front door. There she balked at the tiny step up over the doorframe and down to the porch. Nothing would persuade her to do it. I tried to keep everyone else at bay while he tried over and over to get her out.

Then he asked us to back up further and got her to sit down in a straight chair. Her two tall sons picked it up and carried it and her to the car that would take her back to the place where she could pretty nearly cope, or at least where her limits weren't taxed. It wasn't being carried out in a coffin, but the short procession had for me some sense of grave finality and of tragedy. Another door had shut. Not the last one, but an important one. She wasn't going to go up those stairs again.

My mother was a happy child. Then she was a lost child who fell or lay down regularly. Then she was a person who had trouble finding words and became more and more silent and harder and harder to understand. After that she became more and more tentative about walking and the point at which she would no longer be able to walk approached. I skipped a week because I had a cold and that next stage arrived while I was away. Her legs were fine as far as we could tell, but the panoply of skills and the confidence and will involved had eroded too far. I learned a lot in witnessing

coast story, this one about a chief's son who married a beautiful goose, lost her,

her travel steadily into the unknowns and unknowables and in contemplating what constitutes a self beyond possession of skills and facts, and the value of that self beyond functionality.

Time passed. She was being helped with everything: with getting out of bed, with dressing, with eating, with going to bed, with washing. For her eightieth birthday, early in her second year in the Alzheimer's residence, I'd baked her a cake and had a party at my home up three flights of stairs, but for her eighty-third birthday I brought her a tiny *tres leches* cake and a lunch of small salads and fed her and myself, though she picked up a few bits with her fingers. I lit three candles and one of the workers came over and sang to her with me, but my mother seemed confused by it all and was most definitely not going to blow out the candles. I blew them out and wasn't sure what to wish for on her behalf. But she didn't seem unhappy, even if the bright joy had flickered out a few years before. The road continued onward and downward. Both of us were at peace.

My friend Malcolm told me a story about pronghorns recently, the North American creatures sometimes confused with antelopes. They can run at speeds of nearly sixty miles an hour, much, much faster than any of their existing predators. Some biologists think they're still outrunning the dangerous species that went extinct at the end of the Pleistocene, specifically the cheetahs that existed on this continent. And then Malcolm asked what each of us is still outrunning and whether we can tell when our predator has been extinct for ten thousand years.

She was so many people on the long road downhill. When I read my own old letters in which I talk about her, I see someone I hope I no longer am, someone who didn't see the earliest stages of

searched for her. He had managed to marry her because she took off her skin—in

Alzheimer's as anything more than a new phase of a capricious, demanding personality, though I think I was kinder in person than in the venting letters written after I'd done my best. I read those old e-mails and letters and remember the person who wrote them who no longer seems to be me. I blush, but to look at them is to recognize that I've also metamorphosed.

Sometimes I get mail for people who lived in my home before I did, and sometimes my own body seems like a home through which successive people have passed like tenants, leaving behind memories, habits, scars, skills, and other souvenirs. Even much later, my heart lagged behind, for I was still sometimes struggling against the extinct mothers of bygone years, working out the past, or working over the past, when the present was something else entirely. It didn't interfere with tending the person who had been pared back to essentials and still had that to teach me. Toward that person I could be entirely solicitous and unguarded.

Neither of those people exist any longer, and they called each other into existence in a peculiar way. My sister-in-law once said I was like an electrical ground; my mother sparked and her current ran into me when I entered the room, and I realized that someone else existed when I wasn't around, someone I never met. I was perhaps also someone she never met. I was obdurate, stern, heavily armored for survival when she was around in those years. I survived, and then everything changed.

When I look back at those decades that she was furious that I was different from her and I was terrified of being like her and trying hard not to be, I see how much alike we were, how much she shaped some of my most essential tastes, interests, and values. She was preoccupied all her life with moral questions and prin-

these tales being a bear, a swan, a serpent, is like wearing a garment, and when

ciples, and thought one's life had to be justified by achievement and contribution, and that I inherited. More ethereal things came too, a pleasure in flowers and the bare branches of trees, in books, a certain kind of restlessness and uncertainty. And of course I looked a great deal like her.

The ancient Greeks used a word, *sungnômé,* that means to understand, to sympathize, to forgive, to pardon, a word that refuses to distinguish between thinking and feeling. It proposes that understanding is the beginning of forgiveness or the thing itself. The scope of this word implies that it takes empathy to try to understand and understanding to reach the empathy that is forgiveness—that they proceed together, helping each other along the way. Or that they were never separate in the first place. We use the word *understanding* that way in English, and a request for forgiveness often asks for understanding (which can veer into peddling excuses).

When I was younger, I studied the men I was involved with so carefully that I saw or thought I saw what pain or limitation lay behind their sometimes crummy behavior. I found it too easy to forgive them, or rather to regard them with sympathy at my own expense. It was as though I saw the depths but not the surface, the causes but not the effect. Or them and not myself. I think we call that overidentification, and it's common among women. But gods and saints and boddhisattvas must see the sources of all beings' actions and see their consequences, so that there is no self, no separation, just a grand circulatory system of being and becoming and extinguishing. To understand deeply enough is a kind of forgiveness or love that is not the same as whitewashing, if you apply it to everyone, and not just the parade through your bed.

they strip naked, it's not so much that they're human, but that they are no longer

Now I see my mother in her prime as a woman driven by unseen forces, unclear on the consequences of her actions, unclear on her own desires and contradictions, hemmed in by the unexamined, suffering and occasionally celebrating: an intricate landscape whose various parts were not acquainted with one another, a labyrinth in which she was lost. It was always clear that her reaction to me came out of misery that flowed through her as a set of conventional stories, commands, values, and standards. We were the worthless gender together.

Vengeance and forgiveness, two of the principal methods of resolution we're offered, seem to me to come out of accounting (and we even say *accountable* to mean responsible and say *forgiven* about monetary debts). It's as though a wrong is a debt, and vengeance collects it. You did something terrible; I do something terrible as payback; the score is settled (in theory, though cycles of revenge have a tendency to be endless). Or I forgive you, and your debt is canceled because of my magnanimity.

Maybe the word *forgive* points in the wrong direction, since it's something you mostly give yourself, not anyone else: you put down the ugly weight of old suffering, untie yourself from the awful, and walk away from it. Forgiveness is a public act or a reconciliation between two parties, but what goes on in the heart is a more uncertain process; suddenly or gradually something no longer matters, as though you have traveled out of range or outlived it. Then sometimes it returns just as you congratulate yourself on its absence.

My mother regretted not going to college, but she did take classes for free for a while when she was a clerical worker at New

so different, and the distance between them can be closed by desire. And the goose

York University in her early twenties. She took bookkeeping classes because it seemed more practical than whatever transformation she yearned for, whatever elevation the word *college* conjured for her. And it was practical; for a decade after her divorce, she was the bookkeeper for a theatrical and modeling agency, keeping accounts in order as beautiful people rushed in and out. She was a bookkeeper in other things as well, in that she expected the accounts to all come out even, and brooded over the old imbalances in the ledgers of life.

She had wanted recompense, fairness, columns of numbers that added up, credit that could be cashed in. Catholicism's economy of sin, virtue, repentance, punishment, and reward still oriented her long after she left the church, but forgiveness is also a powerful force in Christianity. Finally, all that reckoning and accounting faded away, the sense of poverty, the conviction she was owed, the chessboard war. Vengeance and forgiveness are about reconciling the accounts, but accounting is an ugly description of the tangled ways we're connected. I sometimes think everything comes out even in the end, but an end that arches beyond the horizon, beyond our capacity to perceive or measure, and that in many cases those who trespass against you do so out of a misery that means the punishment preceded and even precipitated the crime. Maybe that's acceptance.

One branch of medieval Chinese Buddhists focused on filial piety toward mothers, rather than the fathers at the center of Confucianism. David Graeber describes this perspective in his book *Debt:* "A mother's kindness is unlimited, her selflessness absolute; this was seen to be embodied above all in the act of breastfeeding,

without her feathers could not fly away. Perhaps the stories propose that human

the fact that mothers transform their very flesh and blood into milk. . . . In doing so, however, they allow unlimited love to be precisely measured.

"The kindness of our parents is said to be as vast as the horizon of heaven." These matriphile Buddhists quantified the milk with an arbitrary figure—180 pecks, or about 1,500 gallons—but made its value unquantifiable. The debt was so boundless it could not be repaid and did not have to be—except by donating to the Inexhaustible Treasuries of the monasteries, so that, like Jean Sans-Peur, the mothers would have monks praying for them—saying sutras for them in this case. What I have to say could count as a sutra or another sin.

beings are perpetually naked animals, more a potentiality than an identity. In the

13 · Apricots

Two pints of those apricots from a summer long ago still survive. I live a few miles away from where I did when I canned them, my mother's house from which the apricots came was sold years ago, both of us are different people, and so much has happened, so much has changed, but not inside those glass jars. The fruit as I look at it now on the table before me is a solid deep orange color, halves heaped up on top of each other to the rim of the lid, the syrup still clear, though the length of vanilla bean has disintegrated into black crumbs at the bottom of the jar.

The fruit is in wide-mouth jars whose golden lids are a little dusty, but whose vacuum seal has held. Each jar is full, though not so full that the halves crush or confine each other; they float free in their tiny ocean of sugar water. I no longer know what occasion would be momentous enough to open the jars or who I would feed them to, this fruit from a tree in the garden of a long-gone house, this windfall that arrived one faraway August day.

The two jars before me are like stories written down; they preserve something that might otherwise vanish. Some stories are best let go, but the process of writing down and giving stories away fixes a story in its particulars, like the apricots fixed in their sweet syrup, and the tale then no longer belongs to the writer but to the readers. And what is left out is left out forever.

---

end, after a long quest, the bereft husband of the goose becomes a seagull. The

---

The mountain of apricots that briefly occupied my bedroom floor was so many things besides food. It was a riddle and an invitation; it fed imagination and inquiry first. Upon its arrival it seemed to be an allegory for something yet to happen. A year later that unstable heap seemed like a portrait of my life at that time, my life that also had to be sorted, the delicious preserved, the damage pared away. Processed and turned into jam, preserves, and liqueur, the actual apricots went onward as gifts to the people I was close to and the people who helped me during that era of emergency. I ate some myself and drank plenty of thimblefuls of that liqueur.

But I now see the apricots as an exhortation to tell of the time that began with their arrival. As a gift from my mother, or her tree, they were a catalyst that made the chaos of that era come together as a story of sorts and an invitation to examine the business of making and changing stories and locate the silences in between. "It is only by putting it into words that I make it whole," Virginia Woolf once wrote.

She continued, "This wholeness means that it has lost its power to hurt me; it gives me, perhaps because by doing so I take away the pain, a great delight to put the severed parts together. Perhaps this is the strongest pleasure known to me. It is the rapture I get when in writing I seem to be discovering what belongs to what. . . . From this I reach what I might call a philosophy; at any rate it is a constant idea of mine; that behind the cotton wool is hidden a pattern; that we—I mean all human beings—are connected with this; that the whole world is a work of art; that we are parts of the work of art."

The sudden appearance of the patterns of the world brings a

Ohlone people near me still dance the bear dance, men with black and white lines

sense of coherence and above all connection. In the old way of saying it, tales were spun; they were threads that tied things together and from them the fabric of the world was woven. In the strongest stories we see ourselves, connected to each other, woven into the pattern, see that we are ourselves stories, telling and being told. Stories like yours and worse than yours are all around, and your suffering won't mark you out as special, though your response to it might.

One evening, while listening to a blues program on the radio, I heard the blues musician Charlie Musselwhite tell about how he stopped drinking himself to death. In 1987 a toddler fell down a well in Midland, Texas, and the story of her rescue dominated the news for the fifty-eight hours it took hundreds of rescuers to get her out. Jessica McClure, not yet two years old, stuck twenty-two feet down a well eight inches in diameter, sang nursery rhymes and a song about Winnie the Pooh, while workers frantically drilled through the hard bedrock of her backyard.

Radio personalities talked about her, television news programs swarmed the site and focused obsessively on her plight, and newspapers made it a national front-page story. The event was said to be the accursed birth of cable-network news and round-the-clock news coverage. Musselwhite heard about her on the radio when he was driving to work and thought, "Man! My problems were small compared to hers. Why couldn't I be even half as brave as she's being? I thought 'That's it. Until she gets out, I'm not having another drink.' It was a form of prayer for her from me. By the time they got her out, I was out too." He never drank again.

A physical therapist told me that chronic pain is treatable, sometimes by training people to experience it differently, but the

drawn on their skin, wrapped in bearskins, stepping this way and that, the teeth

sufferer "has to be ready to give up their story." Some people love their story that much even if it's of their own misery, even if it ties them to unhappiness, or they don't know how to stop telling it. Maybe it's about loving coherence more than comfort, but it might also be about fear—you have to die a little to be reborn, and death comes first, the death of a story, a familiar version of yourself.

It was as though Musselwhite forgot himself, got lost in the forest of stories, and came back not so attached to his story. That stopping drinking was his first thought shows how much it was already on his mind. It was as though he had been staring at the door when a key fell through the window, and of course he himself was the prison, the door, the window, and the key. Like a fairy-tale protagonist, he was rescued by his empathy with an even more fragile creature, and if the story of the girl in the well was a ladder out of his own hell, compassion was the force that got him to the ladder and maybe up it. His will to rescue her rescued him.

What the singing child at the bottom of the well means depends on whose life you look at. A photographer got the Pulitzer Prize for his image of the swaddled, injured, dirt-smeared girl being returned to the surface of the earth in a crowd of men in jumpsuits and hard hats. The slender firefighter who got her out was overwhelmed by the attention he received and maybe given no room to be traumatized by what was supposed to be a triumph. His mother collected all the stories of his feats and subsequent honors in a scrapbook he took to throwing across the room.

He had gone headfirst down the parallel hole the rescuers drilled, trapped in a narrow stone passage that pressed on his chest, using lubricant and props to inch the child out of her trap—one account compared him to an obstetrician delivering a child,

and ears and fur and claws of the animal silhouetted against the firelight at night upside down and underground, but he was also like a man who was forced back down the tight passage of birth that was also potentially a grave. After the fanfare died down, his marriage failed, he lost his job because he was strung out on painkillers, and several years later, at the age of thirty-seven, he drove out to his parent's ranch, borrowed their shotgun and some shells, telling his mother he wanted to shoot a rattlesnake, and killed himself.

The story meant something else to the philosopher Peter Singer, who used the incident of the child in the well as an example of the irrationality of our impulses. People moved by the story sent the child at its center money, perhaps as much as a million dollars. The donations didn't get her out of the well, though the money did help her teenage parents move to a better home. The rest of it was put in trust for her to collect when she turned twenty-five in 2011. Singer pointed out that worldwide about 67,500 children died of poverty-related causes during the two and a half days that Jessica McClure was down the well, and the money that didn't save her could've helped them.

He talked about our "two distinct processes for grasping reality and deciding what to do: the affective system and the deliberative system." As he explains it, the former deals in images and stories, and generates emotional responses; the latter works with facts and figures and speaks to the rational, reasoning mind. It's clear which one he values most. But it must be the affective system that brings something to the rational mind, that chooses to listen to a story about a child or 67,500 children, that is convinced they matter and that you must respond.

Stories of suffering and destruction are endless and overwhelming these days, and you cannot respond to all of them. If

when I saw them, so that what was human and what was bear was not so clear,

you don't shut them out entirely, you must choose which to respond to and how to respond via both affective and deliberative processes. The two horses are harnessed to the same wagon; maybe there is only one horse who thinks and feels, and maybe there should be one word for the process too, like the word *understanding* we use to mean forgiving or being aware.

Jessica McClure avoided the public eye, went to college, married, had children of her own, grew old enough to collect her trust fund. Poor children continue to die of preventable causes, and other poor children live because of strangers' kindness expressed in money and involvement. Charlie Musselwhite got out of his well thanks to his empathic involvement in McClure's story. You can't calculate in advance who will be saved, how effect ripples outward. His most recent album, his first entirely of his own material, tells the story of his hell and his salvation. It's called *The Well,* and the tidal rhythms of the title song demand dancing.

The child had fallen down the well because her mother went inside to answer a ringing phone and because someone had removed the well cover. The deus ex machina are all around us, all the time. Julia Princep Jackson Duckworth was happy with her first husband, who one day in 1870 reached up to pick a fig for her, ruptured an abscess, and died quickly of the resultant infection, leaving a widow whose second husband would beget Virginia Stephens and three other children upon her. A phone call, a fig. It almost didn't happen, and then it did, and lives were changed for the worse and the better.

Virginia, the second daughter born of that union brought about by a fig or an abscess or both, grew up, married a kind outsider who gave her the name of a wild animal and began produc-

and perhaps what was both was where we resided that evening, as though we'd

ing a miraculous cascade of books in between her descents into madness. And then came the last descent, a literal one into a river with a big stone or stones in her pocket, when she was already dragged down by grief and dread, by the pain of depression that is in part the fear that the pain will never end. But Virginia Woolf killed herself partly out of compunction, out of unwillingness to put her husband Leonard Woolf through another bout of her suffering, or so her last letter said.

Deus ex machina: there's another story about the way that a methamphetamine user and a mass murderer collided and changed each other's courses. The story seems like a modern *Thousand and One Nights* condensed down to one night, when Ashley Smith of suburban Atlanta talked all night to fugitive Brian Nichols. He had taken her hostage in her home at the end of a day in which he'd escaped from the courthouse where he was being tried for raping his ex-girlfriend, critically injured his guard, stolen her gun, and shot dead his judge, a court reporter, a sheriff's deputy, and later, a federal agent.

He was driving the agent's truck when he crossed paths with Smith in her apartment complex in the middle of the night. She was out and about because she had gone to get cigarettes. At gunpoint, the ex-college linebacker made her lead him into the apartment she'd just moved into, tied her up but didn't gag her, and eventually untied her. She told him over and over again about her young daughter, whose picture was everywhere in the house, how much the child meant to her, how she was looking forward to seeing the child again the next morning, how her death would make the child an orphan. She gave her captor the last of her meth and declined to join him—she never used again after that night.

gone back to the place before we were separate. The Native North American

She also talked to him about her addiction, about how her life had fallen apart, and about what had caused it in part: the stabbing murder of her sometimes abusive, sometimes drug-dealer husband in a fight he'd sought out. He had died in her arms, bloodily. After that she took more drugs and worse ones until she found meth or meth found her. Meth produces enormous euphoria while incrementally destroying the brain's pleasure receptors, making ordinary pleasure more and more impossible and more and more meth necessary to feel good again. It's as though you dug your grave with what you thought were wings. Smith's hair was thinned, her teeth were rotting, her family was fed up, her daughter was in her aunt's custody—though she was beginning to put her life back together when Nichols took her hostage. All her stories were stories of loss, but they were also the currency with which she gambled on a chance to save herself.

Something wonderful happens to you and you instantly look back over your life and see it as a series of fortunate events stretching off into the distance like mountain peaks. Something terrible happens and your life has always been a litany of woe. The present rearranges the past. We never tell the story whole because a life isn't a story; it's a whole Milky Way of events and we are forever picking out constellations from it to fit who and where we are.

Even a constellation of damnation can have its uses, though Smith was going to realign her stars. Nichols asked her if she'd ever been in jail, if she'd ever fired a gun, and she talked about her experiences with both, drawing him in in every way she could with stories and anecdotes and information that might rouse his empathy. She showed him her husband's death certificate to make murder real to him. A born-again Christian, Smith vowed to God

stories are not so convinced that human beings are at the center, or that when you

to change her life if she survived. In the morning, she made the fugitive pancakes and eggs and kept telling her story, a low-rent Scheherazade talking the sultan out of his murderous habits.

Nichols let Smith walk out the door with the unspoken understanding that she'd turn him in. He surrendered willingly that morning, leaving his guns behind. When she returned to the apartment a few days later, she found that he had helpfully hung the huge, heavy mirror over her sofa in the brief time between her absence and his surrender. It was slightly off center. The police took it as evidence. The African-American Nichols had his own story, in which he was a slave in rebellion against an unjust system, and there was something to that story, but it didn't explain his utter lack of empathy, from the brutal rape through the four murders. During his subsequent trial his lawyers argued unsuccessfully that he was insane.

Smith's victory was in telling a story compelling enough that it put his on hold, at least temporarily, long enough for her to save her own life and maybe others', maybe his when he surrendered. Spared the death penalty, he is doing life without possibility of parole. She is a motivational speaker forever revisiting her seven hours as a hostage, the story that is the currency of her new life. Tough though the story may be, she preferred it to the story of her husband's murder that had previously defined her life. Now hers is a narrative of finding common ground across great chasms and of surviving and perhaps preventing the deaths of others. Maybe Christianity with its countless tales of sudden transformations gave her the loom on which to weave it.

Musselwhite saved his life by caring deeply enough, Smith by telling in a way that made someone else care or at least hesitate.

travel you come back again. Moths drink the tears of sleeping birds. The birds

And by being yanked from the grip of her own troubles by the intensity of that ordeal. Listen: you are not yourself, you are crowds of others, you are as leaky a vessel as was ever made, you have spent vast amounts of your life as someone else, as people who died long ago, as people who never lived, as strangers you never met. The usual *I* we are given has all the tidy containment of the kind of character the realist novel specializes in and none of the porousness of our every waking moment, the loose threads, the strange dreams, the forgettings and misrememberings, the portions of a life lived through others' stories, the incoherence and inconsistency, the pantheon of dei ex machina and the companionability of ghosts. There are other ways of telling.

As I was approaching this chapter, I woke up in the middle of the night and thought something I should have written down at the time. The empty shell of it that washed up on the shores of morning was to the effect that sometimes an extraordinary or huge question comes along and we try to marry it off to a mediocre answer. The protagonists of fairy tales and fables embody questions about who we are, what we desire, how to live, and the endings are not the real answers. During the quest and crises of a fairy tale the protagonist is nobody, possessed only of the powers of determination, resourcefulness, and alliance, an unconventional estimation of what matters. Then at the end, the story breaks with its own principles and unleashes an avalanche of conventional stuff: palaces, riches, and revenge.

Part of the charm of Andersen's "Snow Queen" is that Gerda rescues Kay from a queen and brings him back to friendship in attics, and that's enough. Many Native American stories don't quite end, because the people who go into the animal world don't

sleep on, inadvertent givers. The moths fly on, enriched. We feed on sorrows,

come back; they become ancestors, progenitors, benefactors, forces still at work. Siddhartha is rich, thriving, loved, privileged, and protected, and walks out on all of it, as though the story were running backward. He's born an answer and abandons that safe port to go out into a sea of questions and tasks that are never ending.

Essayists too face the temptation of a neat ending, that point when you bring the boat to shore and tie it to the dock and give up the wide sea. The thread is cut and becomes the ribbon with which everything is tied up, a sealed parcel, the end. It's easy to do, and I've done it again and again, sometimes with a sense of betrayal of the complexity of what came before, and sometimes when I haven't done it, an editor has asked for the gift wrap and ribbon.

What if we only wanted openings, the immortality of the unfinished, the uncut thread, the incomplete, the open door, and the open sea? What if we liked the brothers to be swans and the nettles not yet woven into shirts, the straw better than the gold, the quest more than the holy grail? The quest is the holy grail, the ocean itself is the mysterious elixir, and if you're lucky you realize it before you dock at the cup in the chapel.

Pared back to its bare bones, this book is a history of an emergency and the stories that kept me company then, but what is an emergency? If you look up the origin of the word you will be sent to the word *emergence,* and *emergence* leads to *emerge:* an emergency is a sudden emerging. The first definition the *Oxford English Dictionary* gives for *emergency* is the same as for *emergence:* "the rising of a submerged body above the surface of water. Now rare." Then comes "the process of issuing from concealment," as though an emergency was a bather coming out of the reeds, a

on stories, on the spaciousness they open up when they let us travel in

secret come out of a mouth. And then the definition we're used to, "a state of things unexpectedly arising, and urgently demanding immediate action."

An emergency is suddenly coming out of one state and into another, out of water into air, out of stability into turbulence, out of familiarity into strangeness, out of assumptions into questions. It's an accelerated phase of life, a point at which change is begotten, a little like a crisis. Quite a lot of suffering often comes along with it, of mourning for what will be left behind—an old self, an old love, an old order—and of fear for what is to come, of the wrenching difficulty of change itself. The poet John Keats once referred to earth as "this vale of soul-making," and it's in emergencies and difficulties that souls are made. If an emergency is an accelerated emergence, merge is the opposite condition, "to immerse or plunge (a person, esp. oneself) in a specified activity, way of life, environment, etc." or "to immerse or plunge in a liquid" or "to cause to be incorporated, absorbed, or amalgamated."

During the chaos at the end of the apricot summer, I had told a friend my Grand Canyon story, because she had a big decision to make. It was the old story about that trip almost twenty years before, when I had said yes to an invitation to float down the river out of the blue and arrived at my standby motto, "Never turn down an adventure without a really good reason." It was the moment I had overcome the voice of my mother within me, her fearfulness and dutifulness, a landmark moment in my life, even though I had said yes to a trip that didn't take place at the time. At least from it I crossed an internal border and clarified a principle.

Immediately after I told the story, I got a new invitation to float

our imagination beyond our own limits, when they dissolve the boundaries that

down the Grand Canyon from someone I had just met. The trip was two years away, an eternity, and then the time came. A year after I went to Iceland I got on a raft at the head of the Grand Canyon to float down the river. At the end of that trip, I realized that it wasn't my turn to be Job anymore, to be pushed so urgently out of being into becoming. It was my friends' turn: they lost family members, ended relationships, got diagnosed with grave illnesses, and I did my best to stand by them as they had me. Other things changed, romances arrived, work continued, emotions and beliefs shifted and metamorphosed.

Sometimes it seems as though the twenty years between the first invitation and my actually getting into that powerful river was a parenthetical era, as though I had to do all the things I'd done to become the person who would finally step on that raft. On the night before we set out, I checked into the remote little motor lodge where Sophie and I had had breakfast all those years before and where I had expressed that wish to go down the river that the river guides at the next table had overheard. The diner had changed a little but I had breakfast there again, and then we got on the river.

The journey down the Colorado River was both a time in which nothing happened—my everyday life was set aside, and we had no contact with the outside world—and an encounter with the forces of change at their most charismatic. We were never more than a few dozen yards from fast-moving water, and mostly we were on it, in it, or next to it. The river was huge, powerful, dangerous in places, and the flow of water seemed like the flow of time, as though I had left behind the particulars of my life to step into life itself. The splash and gurgle of small waves around us and

confine us and urge us to extend the potentialities of our imperfect, broken,

the oars lifting and dropping and dripping made a constant music that became roars and thunder when we drew near rapids.

The water was a force that even in the gentlest places could swirl you downstream fast and pull a swimmer into the current or under a rock, that even in the tributary streams could be overpowering. Approaching a rapid, the rippling surface of the river smoothed out and then that clear, glassy water swelled and you went up over the swell into a stretch where the water roiled, crashed, exploded. The waves could throw a whole raft and its passengers into the air or arch over to deluge it. One wave hit me so hard it ripped off my hat and sunglasses and slammed me into a piece of baggage hard enough to create lacerations, and then came another calm stretch.

The river changed but never ceased, and this temporary life where I was always near that unbroken continuity was an experience of a particular kind of coherence. The river was a snake we rode or resided next to for all that time, never out of reach of its coolness, its strength, its ability to carve stone, to toss trees high into the rocks, to pull swimmers into its currents, to keep going. The river was an artery into which the red veins and capillaries of the canyon country all drained.

The river itself was green because the red after which it was named came from sandstone sediment that sank to the bottom of the reservoir upstream, where the water also cooled down. The cool green snake we floated on had replaced the warm red one that thrashed its route deeper for millions of years. Once rain fell gorgeously, ferociously, and dust washed down a tributary stream to turn the river red again for a day, and then the next day it was brown, and the day after that green again.

incomplete selves. Those apricots my brother brought me in three big cardboard

Geology was what the guides pointed out most on the trip, the signs of the deep, deep past, back to almost two billion years ago, as we descended more than a mile below the surface of the surrounding earth. The oldest rock was the Vishnu Schist, relic of an archipelago ground down long before the continents assumed their current form. The canyon is nothing if not a stunning example of the power of the weak that is water over the strong that is stone. The side canyons demonstrated this most overtly, those tall narrow canyons through polished walls of stone with a deceptively gentle stream at the bottom.

What most captivated me was that water in the present and the way we floated through a continuously unfolding space, as though we were tiny travelers in a Chinese scroll. What was absent colored experience too: no money, no commerce, no news, no reflections or mirrors except the tiny one in which I checked how I was doing with the smearing of sunscreen each morning, no windows, no doors, no architecture, no buildings, no keys, no locks, no clock, no hours or minutes, no breaking up of the day into disjointed fragments of indoors and out, solitary and crowds, noisy and silent, hot and cold, sunlit and artificially illuminated or dark.

There was nothing to take shelter from, not cold, not danger, and no shelter to take: we lived in the open air all the time, seeking shade, approaching the dangers of the river with prudence but not separating ourselves outright from the world around us. I thought of the Heart Sutra, of the passage, "there is neither ignorance nor extinction of ignorance, neither old age and death, nor extinction of old age and death; no suffering, no cause, no cessation, no path; no knowledge and no attainment." There was an abundance of all kinds of absence and lack.

boxes long ago, were they tears too? And this book, is it tears? Who drinks your

As the river cut through eons of stone, as we descended deeper into the canyon, it grew hotter and hotter. I stopped setting up my little tent and used my sleeping bag only as a pad to lie on. On the last night of the trip it was so hot I couldn't sleep, even lying in just a slip on the high ledge where I had thought I might find a breeze, and so after midnight I slipped on my eternally dirty and damp river sandals and walked down the narrow path through thick dust, past barrel cacti and cholla cacti, past the beautiful mesquite tree bower I'd thought of sleeping in before I realized it was full of red ants, past all the sleepers in their varieties of repose and silence, into the zone where the dusty ground turned into pale sand that settled when the lighter red dust was washed downstream.

The six tethered rafts were lined up in a row, each river guide sleeping on the broad bench of his or her raft, like Thumbelina in her walnut shell or Peach Boy in his peach, but the baggage raft was uninhabited. I waded into the river, keeping the music of my movement through water to a faint sloshing chime, and slowly circumambulated the raft, one hand on its side for safety, a little intimidated by the pure cold mystery of the dark waters that tugged at me as the bank dropped away and I went in deeper. I walked into the river up to my neck and walked out on the other side of the raft, cooler.

---

tears, who has your wings, who hears your story?

Thanks

The poet Antonio Machado writes of dreaming that he had a beehive inside his heart and of the bees making "from my old failures white honeycomb and sweet honey." Failures are easy to come by, and making honey of them is harder, but I've tried with mine. And sometimes I was given honey directly. Gratitude for friendships and kindnesses runs through this book that is among other things a portrait of what made my life rich even when times were rough, but some of them bear repeating: deepest thanks to Fríða for the key to the far north and her friendship and luminous intelligence, and to Elín for the way she entered my work and I hers, to Úlfur Chaka Karlsson, never met but instrumental. Thanks to the Artangel Foundation that funded and manages Roni Horn's Library of Water and funded my stay there; to Roni Horn for a looking-glass house that looks at the arctic; and to the magnificent Klara Stephenson for many things while I was there. To these dear friends: Nellie King Solomon and Ann Chamberlain; to Susan Schwartzenberg, Mike Light, and John Lum, who visited me in Iceland; to Sam Green, Marina Sitrin, Pam Farmer, Mike Davis, Rebecca Snedeker, Astra Taylor, Antonia Juhasz, Kaitlin Backlund, Greg Powell and MaLin Wilson-Powell, Thomas Evans, Rupa Marya, Genine Lentine, Blanche Hartman, Marisa Handler, and many others, and apologies to all who should've been named and are not. To all the other artists, including Ana Teresa Fernandez, Subhankar Banerjee, Olafur Eliasson, Mona Caron, and Yoko Ono, whose work thinks through the material and helps me see. To the storytellers, the fabulists and fairy tale authors, makers of the water in which we all swim, to Aaron Shurin and Tony Cohan for the weeks in Guanajuato in which one of these chapters was written amid walks and conversations and colors; to Vijiya Nagarajan, whose Tamil mother drew columns on my bedroom floor one evening during the most difficult days, blessings and protections in flour and water that were eventually gnawed away by mice; Malcolm Margolin, the greatest raconteur; as always, to the best agent imaginable, Bonnie Nadell, and the ideal editor, Paul Slovak, and to Sara and Michal and Max at *Granta;* to the Deutsche Guggenheim in Berlin for commissioning me to write an essay for the exhibition catalog of True North, some small portions of which are recycled here; and to the National Endowment for the Arts whose grant to me helped open up the time to write this book. To Elizabeth "Betita" Martinez for telling me about meeting Che Guevara; to my nephew Zur for a little help with the Hebrew word *hevel;* to Shokan Jordan Thorn for some theological consultation; to the Zen Girl Gang; to David Graeber for his insights on debt and value; to the woman at Urban Fauna in the Sunset District who demonstrated spinning wool by hand for me; to the Rumsen Ohlone for an invitation to a summer Bear Dance; to my brother David for the load of apricots and much more. And special gratitude to El Tanguero, who mysteriously lost the Kurosawa movie disk halfway through our viewing so that we moved on to watch Pasolini's *Arabian Nights,* which made me tell him what I knew of the form of the *Thousand and One Nights* and then and there conceive the form of this book, soon after launched with his encouragement.

I finished writing this book several months before the death of my mother, Theresa Allen (1928–2012). After she was gone, I felt more strongly the presence of the dark-haired, yearning, thwarted young woman before I existed and the mother I must have clung to as a tiny child. The middle-aged woman who had so confounded me for decades became just one figure among many, and I missed the ancient, gentle, far-gone person who brought up the rear of the parade.